Latino Heroes of the Civil War

Mike Walbridge

J. WESTON
WALCH
PUBLISHER
Portland, Maine

User's Guide
to
Walch Reproducible Books

As part of our general effort to provide educational materials which are as practical and economical as possible, we have designated this publication a "reproducible book." The designation means that purchase of the book includes purchase of the right to limited reproduction of all pages on which this symbol appears:

Here is the basic Walch policy: We grant to individual purchasers of this book the right to make sufficient copies of reproducible pages for use by all students of a single teacher. This permission is limited to a single teacher, and does not apply to entire schools or school systems, so institutions purchasing the book should pass the permission on to a single teacher. Copying of the book or its parts for resale is prohibited.

Any questions regarding this policy or requests to purchase further reproduction rights should be addressed to:

Permissions Editor
J. Weston Walch, Publisher
321 Valley Street • P. O. Box 658
Portland, Maine 04104-0658

1   2   3   4   5   6   7   8   9   10

ISBN 0-8251-3322-X

Copyright © 1997
J. Weston Walch, Publisher
P. O. Box 658 • Portland, Maine 04104-0658

Printed in the United States of America

Dedication

This book is dedicated to my
wife, Sonja, and to the rest of
my family: Karla, Rogelio, and
Michael Elijah.

Credits

Contents

To the Teacher   vii

Introduction
1

What Is a Hero?   2
Latino Heroes in U.S. History   2
Slavery, Manifest Destiny, and the Mexican War   3
Secession and the Start of the Civil War   5
Latinos in the Civil War   6

The Civil War in the East   7

First Battles: Fort Sumter and Bull Run   8
The Bloody Battles of Shiloh and Antietam   8
Lincoln's Emancipation Proclamation   9
Battle of Gettysburg Turns the Tide   9
The End of the War: Sherman's March and Appomattox   9

LATINO HEROES OF THE CIVIL WAR IN THE EAST   10

David Glasgow Farragut:
   First Admiral in U.S. History   10

Loreta Velázquez:
   Soldier, Spy, and Master of Disguise   21

Federico Cavada:
   POW, Author, and Expert Military Artist   34

The Civil War in the West   46

The Civil War in Texas   47
The Confederate Invasion of the New Mexican Territory   47

LATINO HEROES OF THE CIVIL WAR IN THE WEST   49

Santos Benavides:
   Highest-Ranking Latino in the Confederacy   49

Rafael Chacón:
   Union Hero of the Battle of Valverde,
   Westernmost Battle of the Civil War   61

Manuel Chaves:
    Union Hero of the Battle of Glorieta Pass,
    The Gettysburg of the West 73

**Teacher
Guide 87**

Answer Key 88

Multicultural Education for All Students 93

    Bank's Model: Integrating Multicultural Education
        into the Curriculum 93

    Integrating Multicultural Education into the Civil War 94

Strategies for Using This Book with English Learners 95

    English Learners and the Stages of Language Acquisition 95

    Comprehensible Input: Sheltered Social Studies
        Techniques 95

    Comprehensible Output 96

Assessment Project: Latino Heroes Action Comic Book 98

    Scaffolding Step 1—Teacher-Modeled Class Project 98

    Scaffolding Step 2—Guided Group Project 99

    Scaffolding Step 3—Individual Project 100

Teacher Resources for Assessment Project 101

    Time Line of Nineteenth-Century U.S. History 102

    Time Line of Twentieth-Century U.S. History 103

    U.S. Map Template 104

    World Map Template 105

    Comic Book Storyboard 106

    Twentieth-Century U. S. Latino Heroes: Past and
        Present 107

    Books on U.S. Latino Heroes of the Twentieth Century 111

**Appendixes
112**

Appendix A—Web Sites on Latino Heroes 113

Appendix B—Guide to Military Ranks 114

Appendix C—Latinos in the Civil War:
    Congressional Medal of Honor Recipients 115

    Bibiliography 116

    Index 117

    About the Author 119

To the Teacher

Who Should Use This Book?

This is the first comprehensive book about the role of Latinos in the bloodiest conflict ever to take place on U.S. soil. For this reason, I have tried to make it accessible to as wide a range of students as possible. This book was written for the following students:

1. **All students studying the Civil War.** As described in the section Multicultural Education for All Students (page 93), the role of Latinos in this epic conflict has been excluded from most U.S. history textbooks. This book is unique in that it enables the teacher to integrate the detailed contributions of Latinos into a comprehensive Civil War unit. Moreover, many of the biographies in this book contain information about other key events in U.S. history related to the lives of these six heroes: the War of 1812, westward expansion, the Texas War of Independence, the Mexican War, and so on.

2. **All students studying biographies of famous Americans.** Biographies are widely used in many subjects to personalize difficult concepts, to motivate students to develop reading and writing skills, and to promote cultural pride or cross-cultural understanding. The biographies in this book contain detailed information about six Latino heroes' ancestors, childhoods, Civil War contributions, and later achievements. They are thorough enough to be used along with other biographies of famous Americans found in libraries and textbooks.

3. **English learners, or LEP Students.** Intermediate or advanced English learners—especially Latinos—will be eager to read about the role of these six bilingual Latinos in the Civil War. The book will spark an interest in U.S. history and promote cultural pride, while helping English learners enrich their vocabulary and improve their reading, writing, and thinking skills.

How to Use This Book

There are several different ways to approach this book. Each of the six biographies is designed to be used by a whole class, by a group, or by an individual. Each biography contains a glossary of 15 to 20 words that might be difficult for English learners and younger readers. Each biography is divided into three sections: Before the Civil War, During the Civil War, and After the Civil War. Following each biography is a:

- vocabulary crossword puzzle based on the glossary words
- comprehension check divided into Before, During, and After the Civil War sections
- creative project involving writing and/or drawing
- map activity utilizing a variety of map skills

Each biography can be read separately and in any sequence; however, the book flows best if the chapters are read in order. Additionally, since the comprehension questions are divided by section, the biographies can be read one section at a time or divided up within a class or group.

To provide some context, I have included an introduction about the three main topics of this book: heroes, Latinos, and the Civil War. The biographies are divided geographically into two parts: The Civil War in the East and The Civil War in the West. The three biographies in the Civil War in the East are preceded by a short overview of the entire war from Fort Sumter to Appomattox. The three biographies in The Civil War in the West are preceded by a summary of events west of the Mississippi River—primarily Texas and New Mexico. These lesser-known theaters of the war are often referred to as The Far West in other books on the Civil War. These background sections need not be read in order to understand the biographies. Brief descriptions of key battles and events are included in each biography.

The Teacher Guide contains information about using this book with all students as part of a multicultural approach to the Civil War—Multicultural Education for All Students. It also has detailed information about using this book with English learners. However, many of the techniques described in the section Strategies for Using This Book with English Learners (page 95) can be used by many mainstream students as well. For example, scaffolding and cooperative learning, two strategies described in detail in the Teacher Guide, have also proven to be effective with mainstream students.

The final Assessment Project (page 98) can also be used with all students. The only difference is that more proficient English-speaking students can be expected to include more detailed writing in the project.

The time lines and maps were prepared for the Teacher Resources for Assessment Project (page 101), but they can also be used with each biography without undertaking the entire assessment project. The follow-up ideas for researching twentieth-century Latinos are also an excellent resource for all students.

Finally, there are appendixes: Web Sites on Latino Heroes, Guide to Military Ranks, and Latinos in the Civil War—Congressional Medal of Honor Recipients.

Objectives

Because of the multiple uses of this book, I have divided the objectives into three categories: general, social studies, and language arts.

General

Students will

- describe the contributions of Latinos to the Civil War
- gain an appreciation of the United States as a multicultural nation

Social Studies

Students will

- select, organize, and interpret information from written sources
- read and interpret maps
- label events on a map
- make a parallel time line

Language Arts

Students will

- identify vocabulary in context
- use the writing process to compose paragraphs, poetry, and letters
- write a biographical summary
- read for comprehension
- evaluate reasons for people's actions

Introduction

What Is a Hero?

The word *hero* means different things to different people. To some, a hero is someone who makes a personal sacrifice by doing something dramatic and courageous for others—for example, rescuing people from a burning building or risking one's life in battle. Showing bravery in a specific event represents one kind of hero.

But a hero can also be someone who overcomes obstacles or challenges in life to accomplish something over a long period of time. What this type of hero does may not be as dramatic, but it is no less significant. Heroes can be famous role models in entertainment, sports, business, or politics. Or, they can be everyday, ordinary people, such as parents who work all day for their children, or volunteers who help their community.

In this book, the heroes are persons of Latino heritage who showed their heroism through dramatic, courageous action in the bloodiest war ever fought in America: the Civil War. However, there were many other Latinos who did not fight in the war but who, nonetheless, displayed their heroism by carrying on with their daily lives in support of families, friends, and community.

You, too, can be a hero without participating in some dramatic event like a war or disaster. As you read the lives of these six Civil War heroes, think about how you can apply their determination, courage, and sacrifice to your own life.

Latino Heroes in U.S. History

Latinos are people whose heritage can be traced back to Spain or Latin America. These people have played a significant—though largely unrecognized—role in the history of the United States. The earliest explorers of what is now the United States were Latinos. These explorers from Spain (known as *conquistadors*) are common names in U.S. history books. They include Juan Ponce de León, who explored Florida in 1513; Francisco Coronado, who explored the Southwest in 1542; and Hernando de Soto, who was the first European to see the Mississippi River. After that, Latino names do not appear in most U.S. history books until the 1960's, when the lives of Latino leaders such as Cesar Chavez are included. What happened to Latinos between the 1500's and the late 1960's?

(continued)

Latino Heroes in U.S. History

Latinos did not disappear. They continued to build and later defend what is now the United States. In the 1600's and 1700's, Latinos from Spain settled and developed the land that is now Florida, California, Texas, Louisiana, New Mexico, Arizona, Utah, and Colorado. During this time, they built 205 missions and 70 forts throughout North America.

During the American Revolution, Latinos like Juan de Miralles, a Cuban living in Philadelphia, helped get financial aid from Spanish-speaking countries to support George Washington's army. Meanwhile, a Spaniard, Bernardo de Gálvez, captured eight British forts in the Mississippi Valley to contribute to the eventual American victory in 1783.

The next U.S. war, the War of 1812, was also won with the assistance of Latinos. General Andrew Jackson won the decisive Battle of New Orleans with the help of a battalion of Latinos. In addition, Jorge Farragut and his young son, David Farragut, contributed to the U.S. Navy's victories at sea.

In 1821, Florida became a part of the United States. Latinos continued to shape the destiny of the new territory. Latino Joseph Hernández became Florida's first delegate to the U.S. Congress, president of the Florida legislature, and a brigadier general in the war with the Seminoles.

Also in 1821, Mexico won its independence from Spain. Throughout the mid-1800's, Mexicans continued to build cities and towns around the earlier Spanish missions and forts throughout the northern Mexican land that is now Texas and the southwest United States. And, while Anglo settlers were moving west into these lands, many Latinos were moving east into U.S. territory. By 1830, some 20,000 Mexicans were living in Chicago, Illinois.

By the middle of the 1800's, events that forever changed the role of Latinos in U.S. history were unfolding.

Slavery, Manifest Destiny, and the Mexican War

Between 1830 and 1860, the United States began changing rapidly from an agricultural nation to an industrial one. Roads, railroads, and canals connected the new factories and cities. Telegraph lines allowed people to communicate with each other quickly. To an outsider, the United States seemed to have unlimited potential. But there was a major

(continued)

Slavery, Manifest Destiny, and the Mexican War

problem that overshadowed all of this progress: slavery.

Slavery had been legal in the southern United States since the 1600's. But now, more and more people opposed slavery and wanted it ended. Other countries, such as neighboring Mexico, had already ended it. As the United States expanded westward in the mid-1800's, the issue of slavery became even more of a problem.

For many years, there had been an exact balance between northern free states (where slavery was illegal) and southern slave states (where slavery was still legal). The South feared that if new territories acquired from France in the Louisiana Purchase of 1803 entered the United States as free states, the U.S. Congress would have enough votes to end slavery in the South. In 1820, the Missouri Compromise temporarily solved this problem by allowing Missouri to enter as a slave state while Maine came in as a free state, thus keeping the balance. The rest of the Louisiana Territory was divided into free and slave territory.

Then, in 1836, Texas won its independence from Mexico in a brief war in which the right to have slaves—which was against Mexican law—was an issue. But Mexico never accepted the defeat. The United States did not want to allow Texas to enter the United States because

that would upset Mexico and also further alter the delicate balance between free and slave states. But then, another powerful force came along that changed the U.S. position: Manifest Destiny.

Manifest Destiny, a phrase used in the mid-1840's, meant that the United States believed that it had the God-given right to extend its border all the way west to the Pacific. In 1845, James Polk

Advertisement in the Charleston Gazette, *mid-1600's*

was elected president by promising to acquire this land, either by buying it or conquering it. He immediately annexed Texas and tried to buy the rest of northern Mexico. When Mexico refused to sell the land, Polk sent U.S. troops to build a fort in an area of southern Texas that the United States and Mexico had always agreed was Mexican land. Sure enough, a war started in 1846 when Mexican soldiers tried to drive back what they

(continued)

Slavery, Manifest Destiny, and the Mexican War

saw as a U.S. invasion of their country. The war with Mexico ended in 1848, after U.S. troops invaded Mexico City and forced Mexico to sell the United States the land it had always wanted.

But, just as the acquisition of the Louisiana Territory had fueled the debate over slavery, now the vast new territory acquired from Mexico caused major problems for the United States during the 1850's. Some parts of the new land, such as California, became free states. But in exchange, other lands were allowed to vote on whether they wanted slavery. In 1856, the vote in the Kansas Territory led to so much violence that it became known as Bleeding Kansas. Soon, not just Kansas, but the entire United States, became locked in a bloody confrontation over slavery.

Secession and the Start of the Civil War

The intense argument over slavery in the western territories led to the victory of an antislavery candidate for president: Abraham Lincoln. Lincoln won the election in 1860. Many Southerners felt that Lincoln would try to end slavery—not just in the West, but in their own states. So in the next few months, seven southern states, including Texas, decided to secede, or leave, the United States. They started their own country: the Confederate States of America—the Confederacy, for short.

On April 12, 1861, the Confederacy attacked a U.S. fort in South Carolina called Fort Sumter. The 40-hour battle started the long and bloody Civil War.

After that battle, four other southern states seceded and joined the Confederacy. The states that remained were known as the Union—short for the United States. The war between the Union North and the Confederate South lasted four years and resulted in more than 600,000 deaths. Latinos fought and died on both sides in the war.

Latinos in the Civil War

Latinos throughout the United States faced hard decisions about which side to join and support. Latinos in the eastern United States, along with the Anglos, generally joined the side supported by the state in which they lived. However, those who lived in the South who were already in the U.S. Army had to choose between their careers and their hometowns.

In Texas and the Southwest, the decision was even more difficult. *Tejanos* and *Nuevomexicanos*, as Mexicans living in Texas and New Mexico were called, were still angry at the United States for the way the land had been taken from Mexico just a few years earlier. Family and friends had been killed in that war. These Latinos also had suffered prejudice at the hands of many Anglo settlers and had had land taken away by the new American courts.

But, at the same time, many Latinos wanted to show their loyalty to their state's government. They also wanted to prove that they could fight just as bravely as the Anglo soldiers in defense of their homeland. After the government of Texas voted to join the Confederacy, most *Tejanos* showed their loyalty by fighting in the Confederate army. But New Mexico, unlike Texas, was not yet a state. People living there never had to decide if they wanted to secede. So, most of the *Nuevomexicanos* joined the Union army and defended New Mexico from Confederate attacks.

All in all, an estimated 10,000 Latinos fought in the Civil War. About 5,000 came from New Mexico, 3,500 from Texas, and 1,500 from the rest of the United States. There were entire Latino battalions from California, New Mexico, Louisiana, Arizona, and Texas. Spanish-surnamed soldiers fought in almost every major battle of the war.

Although this book focuses on six Latinos heroes who fought bravely in the Civil War, there were many other Latino soldiers who also fought bravely. These six heroes were chosen because there was enough available information to detail their lives before, during, and after the Civil War. Hopefully, this book will inspire researchers to dig deeper and uncover valuable information about other Latino heroes of the Civil War.

The Civil War in the East

David Glasgow Farragut: Before the Civil War   10
                                 During the Civil War   12
                                 After the Civil War   13
  FOLLOW-UP ACTIVITIES: Vocabulary Review: Puzzle   16
                                     Understanding the Biography   17
                                     Creative Project: Making a Family Crest   19
                                     Map Activity: Farragut's Naval Battles   20

Loreta Velázquez: Before the Civil War   21
                                 During the Civil War   22
                                 After the Civil War   25
  FOLLOW-UP ACTIVITIES: Vocabulary Review: Puzzle   27
                                     Understanding the Biography   28
                                     Creative Project: Writing a Paragraph   30
                                     Map Activity: The Battle of Bull Run   32

Federico Cavada: Before the Civil War   34
                                 During the Civil War   35
                                 After the Civil War   37
  FOLLOW-UP ACTIVITIES: Vocabulary Review: Puzzle   40
                                     Understanding the Biography   41
                                     Creative Project: Writing an Acrostic Poem   43
                                     Map Activity: Escape from Libby Prison   45

First Battles: Fort Sumter and Bull Run

The Civil War officially began on April 12, 1861, when Confederate troops attacked Fort Sumter, South Carolina. For the next three months, however, both sides organized their armies and avoided battles.

The Union North felt that the war would be over as soon as they decided to attack the South. They were much richer. They also had a larger population: 22 million versus 9 million in the South. Finally, they had more factories, roads, ships, and railroads. When the North finally attacked on July 21, they expected a quick and decisive victory.

This first battle, known as the Battle of Bull Run, took place in northern Virginia. In the beginning, the battle went as expected. The North looked as if they would win easily. But then a new Confederate brigade, led by Stonewall Jackson, was rushed to Bull Run. Jackson's army drove the Union army out of Virginia. The North knew then that the war would be harder and longer than they had expected.

The Bloody Battles of Shiloh and Antietam

For most of the next year, the Union's strategy was to attack the Confederates where they were weakest: areas west of the Appalachian mountains and the coastal ports. The Union army, led by General Ulysses S. Grant, captured a number of forts in Tennessee and Kentucky in early 1862. At the same time, the Union navy, led by Admiral David Farragut, was capturing and closing down 180 ports throughout the South. Farragut captured the key port of New Orleans, at the mouth of the Mississippi River, in April 1862. After that, the South had difficulty trading for the supplies they needed to fight.

But after these important Union victories came two battles that showed the nation how truly horrible the war would be. In April 1862, the Confederates surprised Grant's army at Shiloh Church in Tennessee. The fighting that followed resulted in each side losing 10,000 men in just two days. Then, on September 17, 1862, the Confederate army, led by General Robert E. Lee, tried to invade the North at Antietam, Maryland. This time, in the bloodiest battle of the war, the two sides lost a total of 26,000 soldiers. The North did succeed, however, in pushing Lee's army back into Southern territory.

Lincoln's Emancipation Proclamation

Five days after the Battle of Antietam, President Abraham Lincoln made a historic announcement. He said that as of January 1, 1863, all slaves in the Confederate states that did not surrender would be freed. Because another word for freedom is *emancipation* and an important announcement is a *proclamation*, this speech is known as the Emancipation Proclamation. Although no states surrendered and therefore no slaves were freed, the announcement made it clear that the end of slavery was near. There were happy celebrations in many cities across the North. But, the war was far from over.

Battle of Gettysburg Turns the Tide

For the first half of 1863, the North continued to have success in the areas west of the Appalachians. However, Lee's army drove the Union army away from the Confederate capital in Richmond, Virginia. These victories led Lee to attempt another invasion of the North. On July 1, 1863, Lee attacked Pennsylvania. The Union army caught up with him at the small town of Gettysburg, Pennsylvania. At first, it seemed that Lee would win the battle. But the Union ended up winning. Lee lost 20,000 men in the three-day battle—5,000 of them in a desperate last-chance attack called Pickett's Charge. Gettysburg showed that the South probably could not win the war.

The End of the War: Sherman's March and Appomattox

For the next year, the Confederates were still able to keep the Union army from capturing any of the major southern cities or catching up with Lee's main army. This changed in late 1863. A Union general named William Sherman gathered an army totaling 100,000 men and invaded the Confederate state of Georgia. By September, he captured Atlanta, the biggest southern city. He then continued all the way to the sea, destroying anything that was in his way. This became known as Sherman's March to the Sea.

In early 1865, the Union army finally captured the Confederate capital of Richmond, Virginia. Shortly afterwards, on April 9, Lee surrendered to the Union at Appomattox Courthouse in Virginia. The long and costly Civil War had finally ended.

Latino Heroes of the Civil War in the East

DAVID GLASGOW FARRAGUT

First Admiral in U.S. History

David Farragut

David Glasgow Farragut is the most famous Latino hero of the Civil War. He is included in many histories of the Civil War, as well as books about great naval battles. A brave and honorable man, he rose to the top of his profession and gained the respect of people throughout the world. He was so well liked that he was asked to run for president of one country and to become king of another.

Before the Civil War

David Glasgow Farragut was born on July 5, 1801, near Knoxville, Tennessee. He was **descended** from a line of Spanish military heroes such as Don Pedro Ferragut, who fought against the Moors in thirteenth-century Spain. Farragut's father, Jorge Farragut, was born in Spain, came to America, and fought bravely against the British during the American Revolution.

When David Farragut was eight, his mother died of yellow fever. Commodore David Porter, a friend of young Farragut's father, offered to adopt one of the five children. David Farragut (who later said he had been impressed by the commodore's uniform) went with Porter. By 1811, Farragut was living at sea as a **midshipman** aboard the *Essex*, a U.S. naval ship.

The war between the United States and Great Britain—the War of 1812—broke out the following year. The *Essex* became involved in a number of battles with British ships. Farragut first **demonstrated** his courage and intelligence during this war.

In August 1812, young Farragut's quick thinking may have saved the whole ship. After defeating a British ship in a battle, the *Essex* took as prisoners dozens of British sailors. In the night, pretending to be asleep, Farragut noticed

(continued)

DAVID GLASGOW FARRAGUT

a number of the prisoners arming themselves and sneaking out to attack the Americans on the ship. Farragut **crept** out and woke Porter, the captain of the ship. Porter was able to awaken the rest of the ship and defeat the prisoners.

In 1813, the *Essex* headed toward South America. Its next war assignment was to capture British whaling ships. In the Pacific Ocean near Chile, the *Essex* succeeded in capturing eight British whaling ships. On his twelfth birthday, Midshipman Farragut was put in charge of one of the captured ships, the *Barclay.* What a birthday present that must have been—becoming captain of a ship. Immediately, Farragut had problems with the captured British captain of the ship. The captain **refused** to take orders from a 12-year-old boy. Instead, he tried to scare the boy into letting him escape with his ship. But Farragut refused to be scared by this much older, more experienced captain. He ordered the ship's British **crew** to follow the *Essex.* He showed the British captain that, even if he was just 12, he was an officer of the U.S. Navy and would not give up command of his ship.

Farragut continued to prove himself a few months later during a major battle in which 58 of his shipmates were killed. At one point in the battle, Farragut saw a cannonball heading toward another sailor. He yelled a warning and then pulled the sailor down. Instead of being killed, the sailor was only **wounded**. Farragut saved his life.

Twelve-year-old David Farragut saved a sailor's life during this battle of the War of 1812.

(continued)

DAVID GLASGOW FARRAGUT

After the war, Farragut tried to balance his education with his love for the sea. In 1819, he was **promoted** to acting lieutenant on the *Shark*. But he was called home to take his final naval examinations. At the age of 22, he was given his first official command—a ship involved in the battles against pirates on the Gulf Coast. For the next 40 years, he commanded many ships in many different places. However, it was on the Gulf Coast that Farragut proved himself a great naval hero during the Civil War.

During the Civil War

Farragut was living with his family in Virginia when the Civil War began in 1861. Shortly later, Virginia **seceded** from the union and joined the Confederacy. Sadly, Farragut had to leave his home and southern friends and move to New York.

Shortly afterward, Farragut was ordered to lead the Union's navy attack on New Orleans, a Confederate city at the entrance on the Mississippi River. This was Farragut's big opportunity to fulfill his dreams from childhood and show his **courage** and intelligence on the seas.

In April 1862, Farragut decided to move his **fleet** of 17 ships past the Confederate forts that defended New Orleans. In a remarkable **feat**, Farragut guided his ships through a bombardment, which he later described as feeling like "all the earthquakes in the world and all the thunder and lightning . . . going off all at once." Having passed the Confederate forts, Farragut captured his prize: the city of New Orleans. After this dramatic victory in the Battle of New Orleans, a Union general congratulated Farragut for the "bold, daring, brilliant and successful passage of the forts by your fleet . . . ."

When President Lincoln heard of Farragut's bravery, he promoted him to rear admiral. This made Farragut the highest-ranking officer in the entire U.S. Navy.

Farragut continued to help capture key Confederate cities along the Gulf Coast and the Mississippi River. This made it very difficult for the Confederate army to receive supplies from other countries during the rest of the war. However, there was one last heavily defended port: Mobile Bay in Alabama. This port was difficult to capture because the Confederates had placed dozens of barrels of gunpowder, called *torpedoes*, in the water. Since most Civil War ships were made of wood, one of these torpedoes could sink it instantly.

In January 1864, Farragut received orders to attack Mobile Bay. The first ship in his fleet, the *Tecumseh*, was struck by a torpedo and sank in just seven minutes. The sailors on the other ships watched in horror as all but six men drowned. Going ahead, despite the setback, Farragut ordered his ship to take the lead. He bravely shouted, so all could hear, "Damn the torpedoes! Full speed ahead!" This became one of the greatest

(continued)

DAVID GLASGOW FARRAGUT

battle cries in history. It succeeded in inspiring Farragut's men to defeat the Confederate ships and capture the last

port on the Gulf Coast. With this second courageous victory, Farragut became a national hero. He was promoted to vice admiral. The Battle of Mobile Bay is considered one of the most famous battles in naval history.

Shouting "Damn the torpedoes! Full Speed Ahead!" Admiral Farragut captured the last Confederate city on the Gulf of Mexico in the Battle of Mobile Bay.

After the Civil War

Farragut's two key victories were so important to the Union's Civil War triumph that the U.S. Congress wanted to give him a special honor. Since vice admiral had been the highest rank at the time, they had to create a new title: admiral. In 1866, David Farragut became the first full admiral in U.S. history.

By the spring of 1868, Farragut was so popular that he was asked to run for president of the United States. He turned down the **request**. He said he was trained for war, not politics. Another Civil War hero, Ulysses S. Grant, ran instead. He was elected president. Had Farragut run, he might have become the first Latino president of the United States.

(continued)

DAVID GLASGOW FARRAGUT

Farragut never forgot his Latino **heritage**. He continued to speak fluent Spanish throughout his life. While leading a fleet of U.S. ships to Europe, he spent time in Spain investigating his family's history. He found a **crest** used by many of his ancestors that was shaped like a horseshoe. He found that his name came from the Spanish word for horseshoe: *ferradura* or *herradura*. He brought the family crest up to date by adding a fleet of battle ships. Farragut was so honored in Spain that when the queen was overthrown in 1868, a newspaper suggested that Farragut should become the country's new king. Thus, in one year, Farragut was asked to be a president of one country and a king of another.

On August 14, 1870, Farragut died in his sleep in Portsmouth, New Hampshire. He has been remembered as one of the bravest men in naval history. His statue can be found in New York and Washington, D.C. Many paintings of his most famous battles are in museums around the nation.

Many naval officers over the years have studied Farragut's decisions during the naval battles of the Civil War. Before a famous battle in the Spanish-American War of 1898, Admiral George Dewey asked himself, "What would Farragut have done?" There can be no greater compliment for this heroic first admiral of the United States.

The Farragut Statue in Farragut Square, Washington, D.C., is one of many memorials to this naval hero.

DAVID GLASGOW FARRAGUT

GLOSSARY

refused	did not accept something
crew	people working together on a ship or other location
wounded	injured, but not killed
promoted	raised to a higher rank or job
seceded	withdrew from a group, organization, or country
courage	quality of being brave
fleet	a group of ships, trucks, etc., under one control
feat	a difficult action showing skill or bravery
port	a city with a harbor where ships load or unload cargoes
request	something asked for
heritage	cultural traditions from the past
crest	a picture or symbol of one's family heritage
descended	passed from an earlier to a later time
midshipman	student in training to be a naval officer
demonstrated	showed clearly
crept	moved slowly and quietly

Name _____

Date _____

DAVID GLASGOW FARRAGUT

Vocabulary Review

Word List

courage

crest

crept

crew

demonstrated

descended

feat

fleet

heritage

midshipman

port

promoted

refused

request

seceded

wounded

Across

3. His _____ to get a drink was turned down.
4. The construction _____ took a break for lunch.
7. The student _____ how to solve the problem.
9. The _____ of trucks left the factory on time.
10. The late student _____ into the classroom.
13. Making four goals in one game was an incredible _____.
14. The cashier was _____ to manager.

Down

1. The _____ soldier was sent to the hospital.
2. The students talked to their families about their cultural _____.
4. The family hung their _____ on the wall.
5. The southern states _____ from the Union.
6. The naval officer began her career as a _____.
7. He was _____ from many great artists.
8. The teacher _____ to let me get a drink of water.
11. The ship came into the _____ to pick up the passengers.
12. The soldier was awarded a medal for _____ under fire.

       Latino Heroes of the Civil War

DAVID GLASGOW FARRAGUT

Understanding the Biography

 ## *Before the Civil War*

1. Name two of David Farragut's ancestors: _____

   _____

2. What was Farragut's first position in the navy? _____

   _____

3. Describe how Farragut showed his bravery during the War of 1812.

   _____

   _____

   _____

4. Do you think young Farragut would have gone to live with the Porter family if Porter had not been a naval officer? Explain why or why not.

   _____

   _____

   _____

During the Civil War

1. Name the two most important southern cities captured by Farragut.

   _____

2. Who was the president of the United States during the Civil War?

   _____

(continued)

DAVID GLASGOW FARRAGUT

Understanding the Biography

3. How were the Battle of New Orleans and the Battle of Mobile Bay

similar? _____

_____

_____

4. How do you think the sailors felt during the Battle of Mobile Bay?

How do you think they felt afterwards? _____

_____

_____

_____

★ After the Civil War

1. How old was Farragut when he died? _____

2. What did Farragut do in Spain that showed he cared about his

Hispanic heritage? _____

_____

_____

3. What special honor did the U.S. Congress give to Farragut? _____

_____

4. Do you think Farragut would have made a good president? Explain

why or why not. _____

_____

_____

DAVID GLASGOW FARRAGUT

Creative Project:
Making a Family Crest

Admiral David Farragut was interested in his family crest. Often these crests were painted on shields and carried into battle. Use the shield outlined here to design your family crest. Add drawings, symbols, shapes, and designs that reflect your family's history.

Name _____

Date _____

DAVID GLASGOW FARRAGUT

Map Activity:
Farragut's Naval Battles

The map on this page shows the major Confederate cities along the Mississippi River and the Gulf of Mexico. With the rest of the South blockaded by the Union navy, this was the only way the South could get supplies from other countries to their troops. Admiral David Farragut helped to defeat the South in many of these battles.

1. Color all the water on the map blue.

2. Color each state a different color.

3. What two forts did Farragut have to go past to capture New Orleans?

   _____

   _____

4. When was New Orleans captured?

   _____

5. What was the last Confederate city

   along the Mississippi to fall? _____

   When? _____

6. The last Confederate city along the Gulf Coast to fall was Mobile. Find out the date it fell and write it on the map.

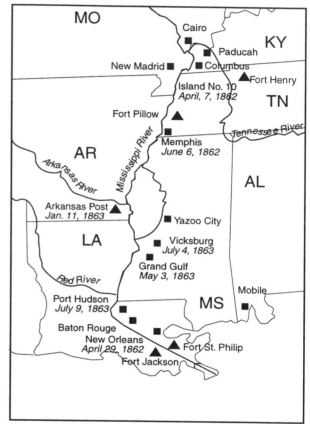

7. Draw an arrow showing the route of Farragut's fleet during the Civil War.
   (a) First, he captured New Orleans.
   (b) Next, he went up the Mississippi River to Vicksburg.
   (c) Finally, he went back down the Mississippi and over to Mobile for his last battle.

8. Why do you think Farragut's fleet could not go farther up the Mississippi?

   _____

   _____

LORETA VELÁZQUEZ

Soldier, Spy, and Master of Disguise

*Because women were not allowed in the army during the Civil War,
Loreta Velázquez had to disguise herself as a man in order to fight.*

*Few veterans of the Civil War led a life as varied and interesting as this **courageous** and determined nineteenth-century woman. **Defying** customs of the times, she made her mark not only as one of the few women to fight in this **epic** war, but also as a daring spy who risked her life on secret **missions** behind enemy lines. Finally, she went on to become a world traveler and author of the book* The Woman in Battle.

Before the Civil War

The father of Loreta Velázquez was born in Spain and educated in Paris, France. He was descended from a famous Spaniard: Don Diego Velázquez, the military governor of Cuba who sent Cortés to Mexico in 1510. Following in the footsteps of this great **ancestor**, the father of Loreta Veláquez moved to Cuba, but chose to be a **diplomat** instead of a soldier.

Loreta Janeta Velázquez was born in Havana, Cuba, on June 26, 1842. When she was just one year old, her father **inherited** a large farm in northern Mexico. He moved his family there. **Ironically**, this man whose ancestor had helped conquer Mexico now found himself involved in another war of conquest against Mexico—this time by the United States. Much of the Velázquez family's property was destroyed in the

(continued)

LORETA VELÁZQUEZ

war. When the war officially ended in 1848, the Velázquez land became a part of the United States. The family decided to return to Cuba.

In 1849, the family sent their daughter to a school in New Orleans, Louisiana, to continue her education. There, young Velázquez learned English and began to dream of her future. Perhaps because of ancestors like Don Diego, she always wanted to be a soldier. So, while her classmates were spending their spare change on candies and cakes, Velázquez was buying books about kings, princes, and soldiers. Her heroine was Joan of Arc, a Frenchwoman who won many battles before her country turned against her, doubting that a woman could be successful as a soldier. Accused of using witchcraft to win battles, Joan of Arc was burned at the stake. Velázquez later wrote of her heroine:

> *From my early childhood, Joan of Arc was my favorite **heroine**; and many a time has my soul burned with an overwhelming **desire** to **emulate** her deeds of **valor**, and to make for myself a name which, like hers, would be enrolled in letters of gold among the women who had the courage to fight like men—ay, better than most men—for a great cause, for friends, and for fatherland.*

In New Orleans, Velázquez met and planned to marry a young U.S. Army officer. Her parents objected because, according to the traditional Spanish customs, they should choose the man she was to marry. Her father was also angry because her husband-to-be was a member of the army that had destroyed his property in northern Mexico. Nevertheless, Velázquez secretly married the officer in 1856 and moved with him to St. Louis, Missouri. There, she continued to study military books and dreamed of someday joining her new husband in battle. When the Civil War started in 1861, Velázquez began to think of a way in which she could fulfill her dreams.

During the Civil War

The husband of Loreta Velázquez had always been unsure about which side he should take in the Civil War. He was born in Texas, which was part of the South. Like many other Southerners in the U.S. Army, he was divided between his career with the Union and his family's loyalty to the Confederate South. Velázquez, having been raised in the South, convinced her husband to quit his job with the Union army and join the Confederate army. As soon as he went east to begin training for battle, she **devised** a plan to join him. Since women were **prohibited** from being soldiers, she decided to **disguise** herself as a man.

Velázquez went back to New Orleans in early 1861 to carry out her plan. First, she had a **tailor** sew a special, padded uniform which made her waist appear larger and more masculine. Then, she had a barber cut and style her hair to look more like that of a man. (She

(continued)

LORETA VELÁZQUEZ

managed to talk him out of giving her a shave!) Next, a trusted male friend helped her glue on a false mustache. He also helped her practice disguising her voice and feminine **mannerisms**. Finally, she selected the name Lieutenant Harry T. Buford, CSA. The change was complete.

The next step in her plan was to **recruit** soldiers to turn over to her husband's command. She visited a small southern town, and within a few days, she had successfully recruited and begun training 236 local men to travel with her to her husband's post in Pensacola, Florida. Her arrival both surprised and angered Velázquez's husband. But she convinced him that he could not reverse her decision. So, he reluctantly agreed to take over the training of the new soldiers. Tragically, he was killed shortly afterward in a gun-training accident.

Despite her sadness and **grief**, Velázquez decided she would continue to pursue her dream of being a military hero. She headed to Virginia, where the war was beginning.

In Virginia, Velázquez found herself immediately caught up in the first major battle of the war—the famous Battle of Bull Run. When she arrived, the Confederate army was badly in need of commanders, so she was temporarily made a company commander under General Bee. Of July 21, 1861, the morning of her first battle, she later wrote, "Fear was a word I did not know the meaning of." Even when she found herself in the middle of the bloodiest part of the battle, with friends dying around her, she continued to fight on. She continued to travel around in search of battles to prove her bravery.

Velázquez fought as well as any man in the Battle of Ball's Bluff in late 1861 and in the Battle of Fort Donaldson in February 1862. But, her luck ran out at

Loreta Velázquez, disguised as Harry Buford, was wounded by an exploding shell at the Battle of Shiloh.

(continued)

23 *Latino Heroes of the Civil War*

Loreta Velázquez

the Battle of Shiloh in April 1862. Shiloh was one of the bloodiest battles in American history, with 23,000 soldiers killed. **Shells** continued to drop while Velázquez and the other surviving Confederate soldiers buried the dead after the battle. One shell landed near Velázquez, severely injuring her arm and shoulder. Despite the **intense** pain, she rode her horse 15 miles to the nearest town. There, a doctor attending to her wounds became suspicious of her identity. Realizing that she was caught, Velázquez confessed that she was a woman. She wrote of the doctor's reaction, "I never saw a more **astonished** man in my life."

Despite the discovery of her disguise, Velázquez was determined to participate in the war. While she was recovering in New Orleans, Admiral Farragut captured the city for the Union. Finding herself now in enemy territory,

she traveled back to her birthplace—Havana, Cuba—where she was delighted to hear her native tongue, Spanish, being spoken. In the summer of 1862, Velázquez met with Confederate officers. Then she returned to New Orleans, where she was arrested for spying. As soon as she managed to get away, she disguised herself and headed north. proved their valor during the Civil War—much as Velázquez had in the eastern United States.

In 1876, Loreta Velázquez wrote a detailed description of her adventures, *The Woman in Battle*. Many readers of this book were shocked to find out the true identity of Lieutenant Harry T. Buford, CSA.

In the fall of 1862, Velázquez decided to drop her disguise to see if she could obtain important information about the war. Dressed as a woman, she traveled to Washington, D.C., the Union capital. There, she met an old military friend, who took her to meet with top government official—including

Whenever Valézquez returned to her homeland, Havana, Cuba, she was happy to hear Spanish spoken everywhere.

(continued)

LORETA VELÁZQUEZ

President Lincoln himself. Unable to find out much important information, she returned to the battlefield. Her career as a spy, however, was not over.

In 1864, Velázquez began her new career as a spy for the Confederate army. The South was losing badly in the war and planned a surprise attack against the Union in the northern Great Lakes area. There, the Union had a large camp with a large number of Confederate prisoners of war. The plan was to help these prisoners escape and provide them with weapons to carry out attacks along the lakes. All the South needed was a way to communicate the plan to the prisoners inside. Velázquez, who had convinced the North that she was on their side, went to a Union colonel and told him parts of the plan. She got permission to go to the prison to try to find a Confederate spy inside. Of course, she was the real spy, using the search for a spy as an excuse to get in and tell the prisoners about the South's plan! Velázquez played her part perfectly. She got inside, told the prisoners about the plan, and gave them money. But, in the end, the plan failed.

Velázquez continued to travel around the North in various disguises. She carried out different missions as a spy without being caught. When the war ended, she returned to the South.

After the Civil War

Having spent so much of her youth wrapped up in the tragic events of the war, Velázquez now decided to spend some time traveling to places she had once read about. In 1865, she traveled through Europe with her brother. In Paris, she met a number of ex-Confederate officers who commented on the bravery of a woman disguised as a male soldier and a spy—without knowing they were talking to Loreta Velázquez herself. Afterward, she visited Venezuela and then traveled throughout the Caribbean area. She ended up back in Havana, Cuba. There, a military friend insisted that she be allowed to march in a military parade. So, dressed again in the uniform of her Civil War days, she marched with other soldiers right by a U.S. diplomat, without being recognized.

Returning to the United States, Velázquez was still unable to sit still. She decided to travel west, as many others were doing after the war. She arrived in a Nevada mining town in 1868 with a new husband to start a new life. From there she continued to travel throughout Colorado, New Mexico, and Texas. She passed through some of the same areas where other Latinos had proved their valor during the Civil War, much as she had in the eastern states.

In 1876, Loreta Velázquez wrote a detailed description of her adventures, *The Woman in Battle*. Many readers of this book were shocked to find out the true identity of Lieutenant Harry T. Buford, CSA.

LORETA VELÁZQUEZ

GLOSSARY

courageous	brave
defying	resisting openly and bravely
epic	long and heroic
missions	special jobs or duties one is sent out to do
ancestor	a person from whom one is descended
diplomat	representative of a government
inherited	received from a relative who died
ironically	being opposite of what is expected
heroine	girl or woman hero
desire	a wish or craving
emulate	to try to copy
valor	courage or bravery
devised	planned or invented
prohibited	not allowed; forbidden
disguise	make to appear different
tailor	one who makes, repairs, or alters (changes) clothes
mannerisms	ways of speaking or behaving
recruit	get someone to join a group or army
grief	deep sorrow or sadness over a loss
shells	bombs or missiles fired from a large gun
intense	very strong
astonished	suddenly surprised

LORETA VELÁZQUEZ

Vocabulary Review

Word List

ancestor	heroine
astonish	inherited
courageous	intense
defying	ironically
desire	mannerisms
devised	missions
diplomat	prohibited
disguised	recruit
emulate	shells
epic	tailor
grief	valor

Across

3. When her dog died, she felt sadness and _____.
5. The _____ exploded all around them.
8. It was very _____ of you to go on the roller coaster.
11. I _____ a plan to study for the test.
12. The _____ movie was too long for the young kids.
14. The U.S. _____ had to live in many countries.
17. My _____ to eat ice cream became overwhelming.
19. _____, the fire station burned down!
20. I took my pants to the _____ because they were too long.
21. I wanted to _____ my mother by getting perfect grades.
22. Her _____ helped me understand what she was saying.

Down

1. I was _____ from opening the presents before the party.
2. The astronaut went on four _____ into space.
4. We needed to _____ more members for our club.
6. The student was suspended for _____ school rules.
7. I _____ a million dollars from my grandfather.
9. Do you have a famous _____?
10. Do you have a hero or _____?
13. I tried to _____ his hairstyle, but it came out different.
15. She showed her _____ by finishing the long race.
16. The children were _____ in great Halloween costumes.
18. The game was so _____ that both teams were too tired to continue.

| LORETA VELÁZQUEZ |

Understanding the Biography

 ## Before the Civil War

1. What did Velázquez's famous ancestor do? _____

2. Who was Velázquez's childhood hero? _____

3. Describe her dreams when she was a child:

   _____

   _____

4. Do you think Velázquez would have married the man her parents chose or the man she wanted? Explain why.

   _____

   _____

 ## During the Civil War

1. Name the four Civil War battles Velázquez fought in:

   _____

2. What was Velázquez's job with the army after she was wounded?

   _____

3. Describe what Velázquez did to disguise herself as a man:

   _____

   _____

   _____

(continued)

LORETA VELÁZQUEZ

Understanding the Biography

4. After her first battle Velázquez said, "Fear was a word I did not know the meaning of." Do you think she had the same feelings after fighting many battles? Explain why or why not.

_____

_____

_____

⭐ After the Civil War

1. What was the name of the book Velázquez wrote about her life?

_____

2. Why did Velázquez decide to travel so much after the war ended?

_____

_____

3. Name four western states that Velázquez passed through on her travels.

_____

_____

4. How do you think Velázquez felt marching in a parade in Cuba?

_____

_____

| LORETA VELÁZQUEZ |

Creative Project: Writing a Paragraph

Loreta Velázquez's childhood heroine was Joan of Arc. Think of a person who is a hero or heroine to you. The person could be someone famous, a relative, a teacher, or anyone whom you respect and admire. Follow these steps in the writing process to complete a paragraph about this person.

Brainstorm

List why you think the person is heroic. This is sometimes called *brainstorming*.

My hero or heroine: _____

Reasons why this person is heroic:

1. _____

2. _____

3. _____

4. _____

First Draft

Now take these details and make a paragraph with a topic sentence, using the following guide. The first writing of something is called a *first draft*.

My hero/heroine is _____ .

I think he/she is heroic for many reasons. _____

_____

_____

_____

_____

(continued)

LORETA VELÁZQUEZ

Creative Project:
Writing a Paragraph

Revise and Edit

Next, have someone read your paper and give you suggestions on how to make it better. This step is called *revise and edit*.

Rewrite

Then, rewrite the paragraph, using the suggestions.

_____

_____

_____

_____

Proofread

Now, have someone check it once again for any mistakes. You are having the person *proofread* your writing.

Final Copy

Finally, rewrite your paragraph again very neatly, or use a typewriter or computer. The result is called the *final copy*.

_____

_____

_____

_____

_____

LORETA VELÁZQUEZ

Map Activity:
The Battle of Bull Run

The following page shows part of a battle map that Loreta Velázquez included in her autobiography, *The Woman in Battle*. The book was published in 1876. Use the map to answer the questions below:

1. What three states are shown?

   _____

   _____

   _____

2. Find the site of the Battle of Bull Run, and then find Washington, D.C. Circle them in red.

3. Use the scale at the bottom of the map to estimate the distance McDowell's Union troops traveled from Washington, D.C., to the site of the battle in 1861:
   _____ miles

4. In addition to the routes of the Union and Confederate armies, three other features are shown on this map: mountains, rivers, and railroad tracks. Color the rivers blue, the mountains yellow, and the railroads brown. Then, add the symbol and color used for each of these features to the following Map Key.

<table>
<tr><td colspan="2">Map Key</td></tr>
<tr><td>Feature</td><td>Symbol</td></tr>
<tr><td>mountains</td><td></td></tr>
<tr><td>rivers</td><td></td></tr>
<tr><td>railroads</td><td></td></tr>
</table>

(continued)

LORETA VELÁZQUEZ

Map Activity:
The Battle of Bull Run

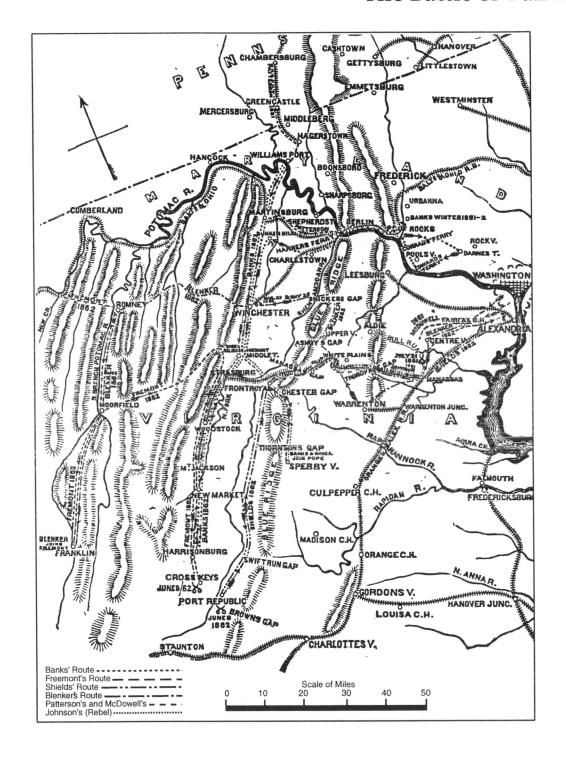

Banks' Route - - - - - - -
Freemont's Route —— - ——
Shields' Route ———————
Blenker's Route —·—·—·—
Patterson's and McDowell's — — —
Johnson's (Rebel) ·············

Scale of Miles

0   10   20   30   40   50

FEDERICO CAVADA

POW, Author, and Expert Military Artist

One of the few pictures of Federico Cavada

*During his short life, Federico Cavada played an important role in both the U.S. Civil War and Cuba's Ten Years' War (1868–78). But it was not only as a soldier and military leader that this remarkable bilingual hero **distinguished** himself. He was also a successful artist, poet, author, diplomat, and **engineer**, whose courage and intelligence **impressed** the leaders of two countries.*

Before the Civil War

The father of Federico Cavada, Don Isidro Fernandez Cavada, was sent by the King of Spain to work in the government of New Spain. He moved to Cuba after New Spain won its independence from Spain in 1821 and became Mexico. In Cuba, he met Emelie Houard. Federico Cavada was born to them on July 8, 1831, in Cienfuegos, Cuba.

The boy's happy childhood in Cuba was cut short by the tragic death of his father in 1838. His mother decided to move the family to Philadelphia, Pennsylvania, to live with her brother. Federico's mother had been born in Philadelphia and had lived there until her family moved to Cuba in the 1820's.

Federico Cavada now found himself an immigrant in a strange and different culture, surrounded by people who didn't speak his language, Spanish. Young Cavada responded to this challenge with the same determination that made him a hero later in his life. He worked hard to learn English and **excelled** at school. At the same time, he never stopped speaking Spanish and always kept a strong attachment to his **beloved** Cuba. At the age of 15, he had a poem about Cuba published in a local newspaper. In the poem, called "The Cuban's Adieu to This Native Land," he predicted that Cuba would someday be independent from Spain:

> *Adieu to thee! Isle I hold dear,*
> *'Till thy people at Liberty's call,*
> *By causing **Iberia** to fall*
> *'Neath the flag of the free shall appear.*

In this poem, he was saying good-bye to Cuba. Yet, 30 years later, Cavada returned to his native land and helped take steps toward the freedom mentioned in the hopeful poem.

(continued)

FEDERICO CAVADA

In 1850, Cavada graduated from high school. He decided to study engineering and map drawing. His first job was with a Philadelphia engineering company called E.H. Hern and Brother. Then, in the late 1850's, he traveled to Panama to help with the construction of a railway line connecting the Pacific Ocean and the Gulf of Mexico. One of his jobs was to use an aerial hot-air balloon to map out the best railroad routes through the jungle. Unfortunately, the **isolated** jungles of Panama were full of many tropical diseases. When Cavada returned to Philadelphia in 1861, he was extremely weak from **malaria** and fever.

During the Civil War

Just as Cavada was returning from his adventures in Panama, the Civil War was exploding. Even though he was in

poor health, Cavada volunteered to fight on July 20, 1861—the day before the Battle of Bull Run. His desire to serve despite his illness greatly impressed his commander, Colonel David Birney. Birney decided to make Cavada a captain in the Army of the Potomac, part of the Union Army.

Soon after joining the army, Cavada was given a special assignment. He was told to **sketch** battles from a hot-air balloon—just as he had sketched railroad routes in Panama. The balloons were called "the eyes of the Army of the Potomac." Cavada floated above battlefields; he used his mapping and drawing skills to create a picture of the battle below. His observations and drawings helped the army respond to Confederate troop movements.

In addition to his aerial artistry, Cavada also participated on the battlefield. Because of his skill with horses, he

Cavada made sketches of battles in the Civil War from a balloon like this one.

(continued)

FEDERICO CAVADA

joined the **cavalry**. In 1862, he fought bravely in combat at the Battles of Chantilly, South Mountain, Harper's Ferry, Antietam, and Fredericksburg. His courageous performance earned him a promotion to major, and then lieutenant colonel.

The Battle of Antietam in Maryland and the Battle of Fredericksburg in Virginia were among the bloodiest in American history. In each of these battles, the Union army lost more than 12,000 men in one day. Cavada was in the thick of the Battle of Fredericksburg when the Union general made the terrible decision to charge the Confederates' position on Marye's Heights. Most of the Union's 12,000 deaths came during this useless attack. Later, Cavada painted the scene of this battle. The painting, *The Battle of Marye's Heights,* hangs today in the Pennsylvania Historical Society Museum. It appears in many books and encyclopedias.

In 1863, Cavada continued to participate in some of the most famous Civil War battles. He was at Chancellorsville in Virginia in May and at Gettysburg in July. At Gettysburg, a **pivotal** Union victory, he was put in charge of the 14th Pennsylvania Regiment because its colonel was not available. General George Meade had recommended that Cavada be promoted to full colonel after the battle. But, in the middle of the

Cavada's painting of the disastrous Battle of Frederickburg appears in many books and articles about the Civil War.

(continued)

FEDERICO CAVADA

battle, Cavada and 2,000 other Union men were captured by the Confederates.

From July 1863 to March 1864, Cavada was held prisoner at Libby Concentration Camp in Richmond, Virginia. It was a prison for captured Union officers. In order to withstand the suffering and boredom of prison life, he turned to writing about his daily experiences. He also drew pictures to go with the writing. He had to write and draw in secret on whatever **scraps** of paper he could find, and then hide the writing in his shoes and socks. In 1865, Cavada writings and drawing were made into a book called *Libby Life*. All the money he made from the book was given to the **widows** of the 20 prisoners who died at the crowded Libby prison when Cavada was there.

The book is filled with evidence of Cavada's talent as an artist and writer. A sketch of a tunnel through which 115 prisoners escaped shows how **precise** he must have been when sketching military battles from the sky. The clear writing in the book shows how well this Cuban-born hero learned English during his schooling in Philadelphia.

In March 1864, Cavada was released from Libby in a prisoner exchange. Despite his weak condition, he returned to the army. Once again he served with David Birney, but now his friend had become a general. Cavada's last Civil War battle was during Grant's Wilderness Campaign in the spring of 1864.

Birney died during one of these battles, and Cavada wrote a poem about their friendship, called "Birney's Grave."

After the Civil War

After spending five years suffering in the long and bloody Civil War, Cavada wanted to find somewhere peaceful to rest and recover. What better place than the country of his childhood—Cuba? In 1866, Cavada's wish to return to Cuba was fulfilled when the U.S. government sent him there to serve as a diplomat. Instead of finding peace, however, he found himself drawn into another war.

At the time, Cuba was still a colony of Spain. Cavada grew angry at the refusal of Spain to grant Cuba's independence. Most of the Spanish empire in the Americas had already gained independence. Cuba was one of the few remaining colonies. Cavada was also upset about the continued use of slavery at U.S. sugar plantations in Cuba. Having suffered greatly in the war that ended slavery in the United States, he decided he could not continue to serve as a U.S. diplomat under these conditions. He **resigned** in 1869.

A war of independence (later known as the Ten Years' War) had started the year before. Cavada wanted to put to use his military experience from the United States. He bought a hacienda called *Las Bocas* and used it to begin training local Cubans to fight against Spain as part of this new Cuban independence movement. At *Las Bocas*, Cavada developed a new kind of fighting called guerilla

(continued)

FEDERICO CAVADA

warfare. In guerilla warfare, hidden soldiers attack the well-organized government troops of a country and then run away; they hide before the government troops can respond. These hit-and-run attacks worked extremely well in the part of Cuba with mountain jungles. Cavada wrote a training manual to be used by all Cubans wanting to learn these new methods of fighting against Spain.

Because of the great success of his guerilla warfare, Cavada became commander-in-chief of the entire Cuban Revolutionary Army in 1870. Under his command, the army continued to grow in strength and captured several important Spanish forts. Cavada was wounded during one of the battles. However, after a three-month recovery, he returned to lead his "**phantom**-like army."

In 1871, the rebels realized that they needed more weapons to continue the war. So, Cavada went on a dangerous mission to obtain arms. He sailed to a neighboring island in a small boat. Cavada could have waited for a safer moment. But he chose to leave early because one of his soldiers, Admiral Osario, was seriously wounded and in need of medical attention. Right after leaving, a Spanish battleship spotted the boat and chased it to shore. Although all of the other men escaped into the mountains, Cavada decided he could not leave his wounded friend Osario. He

stayed with him instead of fleeing and saving himself. As a result of this brave act of **loyalty**, he was captured by the Spanish.

For the second time in his life, Cavada found himself behind bars. This time, however, he was immediately scheduled to be **executed**. News of his capture quickly reached his military friends in the United States. They organized a campaign to pressure Spain to spare his life. Among those sending messages to Spain were Civil War Generals McLellan, Meade, and Burnside. Finally, Secretary of State Hamilton Fish wired an urgent message from President Ulysses S. Grant, who had been the Union's top general in the Civil War. The message demanded that Spain stop the execution. Unfortunately, all of these messages were late. Cavada had already been executed. He was shot by a Spanish firing squad on July 1, 1871, the day after his capture. Just before his death, Cavada threw his hat into the air and shouted, "Goodbye, Cuba, forever!"

The Cuban Ten Years' War ended in 1878, when the government promised to make some important changes, such as the ending of slavery. But, when many promises were broken, the war started again. And this time, the rebels succeeded in freeing Cuba from Spain. Thus, Federico Cavada contributed to the cause of freedom and liberty in two countries during his short but eventful lifetime. He is honored and remembered as a true hero by both the American and Cuban people.

FEDERICO CAVADA

GLOSSARY

distinguished	famous
engineer	one who designs or builds roads, bridges, buildings, etc.
impressed	strongly and positively affected someone's opinion
excelled	did very well
beloved	greatly loved
Iberia	part of Europe containing Spain and Portugal
isolated	set apart, separated
malaria	serious tropical disease spread by mosquitoes
sketch	a quick drawing
cavalry	troops trained to fight on horseback
pivotal	so important it can change the outcome of something
scraps	small pieces of something
widows	women whose husbands have died
precise	exact, almost perfect
resigned	gave up a job or position
phantom	unreal, like a ghost
loyalty	being reliable to friends, family, country, etc.
executed	put to death by law

Name _____

Date _____

FEDERICO CAVADA

Vocabulary Review

Word List

beloved	loyalty
cavalry	malaria
distinguished	pivotal
engineer	precise
excelled	resigned
executed	scraps
Iberia	sketch
impress	widows
isolated	

Across

4. A carpenter must be _____ when measuring.
6. She showed her _____ to the school by going to all the football games.
7. The guest speaker is a very _____ writer.
12. To _____ the teacher, the student tried to get an A on every test.
14. Selena was a popular and _____ singer.
16. Carlos Finlay was a Cuban who helped find a cure for _____.
17. His home run was the _____ hit of the game.

Down

1. The murderer was _____ in the electric chair.
2. The birds liked to eat any _____ of food they could find in the park.
3. The sad _____ never had a chance to say goodbye to their husbands.
5. He _____ when he was offered a better job.
8. Many famous explorers sailed from _____.
9. Hawaii is the most _____ state in the United States.
10. The _____ built the bridge strong enough to survive an earthquake.
11. She _____ in many subjects.
13. The artist made a _____ before starting the painting.
15. The _____ could move faster than the troops on foot.

Latino Heroes of the Civil War

| FEDERICO CAVADA | # Understanding the Biography |

★ Before the Civil War

1. In what year did New Spain become Mexico? _____

2. Where was Cavada born? _____

3. Why did Cavada have to move to the United States? _____

_____

4. Do you think that being bilingual helped Cavada succeed in his job in Panama? How? _____

_____

_____

★ During the Civil War

1. Name the seven battles or campaigns that Cavada participated in.

_____

_____

2. How did Cavada use his engineering skills in the Civil War? _____

_____

_____

3. What did Cavada's famous painting show? _____

_____

_____

(continued)

FEDERICO CAVADA

Understanding the Biography

4. Why do you think Cavada risked his life to write and draw in secret when he was in Libby prison? _____

_____

_____

⭐ After the Civil War

1. Where did Cavada go after the Civil War? _____

2. How did Cavada help Cuba in the war of independence from Spain?

_____

_____

_____

3. Why was Cavada captured by the Spanish? _____

_____

4. Do you think Spain would have let Cavada live had they received the messages from the U.S. before his execution? Explain why or why not.

_____

_____

_____

_____

FEDERICO CAVADA

Creative Project:
Writing an Acrostic Poem

One of Federico Cavada's many talents was writing poetry. He wrote a poem about his home country, Cuba, when he was 15, and he continued to write poetry throughout his life. You can also write a poem about another country or place you have visited. A simple way to write poetry is to use each letter of a topic to begin a phrase about that topic. This is called an **acrostic poem**. This is an example of an acrostic poem Cavada might have written about Cuba:

> **Colorful people**
>
> **Under the burning sun**
>
> **Beautiful beaches**
>
> **A country I love**

Now think of a place you have visited and write an acrostic poem about it:

_____

_____

_____

_____

_____

_____

_____

Have someone read and correct your poem. Then rewrite it, and add pictures on the next page.

(continued)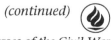

FEDERICO CAVADA

Creative Project:
Writing an Acrostic Poem

————————————————

————————————————

————————————————

————————————————

————————————————

————————————————

————————————————

————————————————

FEDERICO CAVADA

Map Activity:
Escape from Libby Prison

This map/sketch is based on one that Federico Cavada drew for his book about his year in prison, *Libby Life*. It shows a tunnel through which more than 100 prisoners escaped. Use the map to answer the following questions:

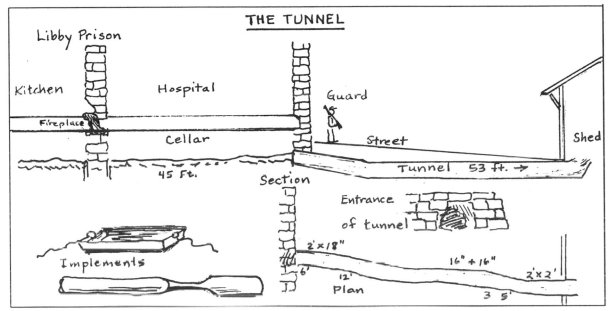

THE TUNNEL

Libby Prison

Kitchen   Hospital   Guard

Fireplace

Cellar   Street   Shed

45 Ft.   Tunnel 53 ft. →

Section   Entrance of tunnel

Implements   2'×18"   16"+16"   2'×2'

6'   12'   3 5'
Plan

Sketch adapted from Cavada's book Libby Life

1. How did the prisoners get from the kitchen to the cellar?

    _____

2. Where did the tunnel lead to? _____

3. According to the upper map, how long was the tunnel? _____

4. According to the lower plan, how wide was the widest part of the

    tunnel? _____ How wide was the narrowest part? _____

5. Describe how the prisoners probably used the two implements (the

    box and the shovel) to dig the tunnel: _____

    _____

The Civil War in the West

Santos Benavides: **Before the Civil War 49**

During the Civil War 51

After the Civil War 53

FOLLOW-UP ACTIVITIES: Vocabulary Review: Puzzle 55

Understanding the Biography 56

Creative Project: Writing a News Article 58

Map Activity: The Civil War in Southeastern Texas 60

Rafael Chacón: **Before the Civil War 61**

During the Civil War 62

After the Civil War 65

FOLLOW-UP ACTIVITIES: Vocabulary Review: Puzzle 67

Understanding the Biography 68

Creative Project: Designing a Poster 70

Map Activity: The Battle of Valverde 72

Manuel Chaves: **Before the Civil War 73**

During the Civil War 75

After the Civil War 78

FOLLOW-UP ACTIVITIES: Vocabulary Review: Puzzle 80

Understanding the Biography 81

Creative Project: Writing a Letter 83

Map Activity: New Mexico in the Civil War 85

The Civil War in Texas

In February 1861, the Texas state government voted to secede, or leave, the United States. Texas decided to join other U.S. states that were leaving to form a new country called the Confederate States of America. Although Texas had very few slaves, it had a history of not taking orders from faraway governments—first, Mexico City, when it was part of Mexico; and later, Washington, D.C., when it joined the United States.

While no major battles were fought in Texas during the war, Texas was important to the Confederacy for other reasons. With the Union Navy, led by Admiral Farragut, successfully blockading the South, the only way the Confederacy could get supplies was from Mexico through Texas. The Texans' job was to protect these trade routes so the soldiers back east could get the supplies they needed to fight.

It was hard, however, to trade with countries in Europe. These countries bought cotton from the South and produced weapons and military equipment the South needed to fight the war. After the U.S. Navy blockaded the Gulf of Mexico, the South could not trade with Europe. The leader of the Confederacy, Jefferson Davis, decided that the only hope for trade with Europe was to capture the West—including the Pacific Coast. Then, the South would be able to trade with Europe through ports such as Los Angeles and San Francisco, California.

The Confederate Invasion of the New Mexican Territory

To capture the Pacific Coast ports considered so important, the Confederates had to pass through the large and mostly unpopulated New Mexican Territory. New Mexico was also all that separated the Confederacy from newly discovered gold mines in Colorado and gold left in California from the gold rush of 1849. So, the desire for trade and gold led the Confederacy to invade New Mexico in 1862. Texas, located right next to New Mexico, was chosen to lead the invasion.

Texans believed that capturing New Mexico would be very easy. The territory had been recently conquered by the United States in the war with Mexico. The territory was still populated by a majority of Latinos, called *Nuevomexicanos*. Many of them were mad at the United States because of the war. So, when Texans entered New Mexico in February 1862, they expected the

(continued)

The Confederate Invasion of the New Mexican Territory

Nuevomexicanos to help them defeat the few Union troops there. But, while a few did help them, the overwhelming majority of *Nuevomexicanos* sided with the Union.

In fact, two of these *Nuevomexicanos* played key roles in stopping the Confederate advance: Manuel Chavez and Rafael Chacón.

The Confederate Texas Army, led by General Henry Sibley, did succeed at first. They captured New Mexico's two largest cities, Santa Fe and Albuquerque.

Then they began moving north toward the gold mines of Colorado. From there, they planned to move west to capture California. But, instead, in March 1862, they were stopped in the Battle of Glorieta Pass. The Confederate plan to invade the West was defeated. The next year, a similar plan to invade the North was stopped at the famous Battle of Gettysburg in Pennsylvania. Because of the similarity, The Battle of Glorieta Pass is called The Gettysburg of the West.

Latino Heroes of the Civil War in the West

SANTOS BENAVIDES

Highest-Ranking Latino in the Confederacy

Santos Benavides in a rare photograph, 1864

Any study of the role of Latinos in Texas during the Civil War would be incomplete without mention of the brave and heroic Colonel Santos Benavides and his Benavides Regiment. Santos Benavides lived his life in an area of southeastern Texas near the Rio Grande. It was an important battleground—not just during the Civil War, but in several other wars throughout the nineteenth century. In each conflict, Benavides showed his valor, intelligence, and leadership. By the end of his life, he had lived under five different flags—the flag of Mexico, the Republic of Texas, the Republic of the Rio Grande, the United States, and the Confederate States of America.

Before the Civil War

Santos Benavides was born in Laredo, Texas, on November 1, 1823. His great-grandfather, Tomás Sanchez, had founded the town of Laredo in 1754, when Texas was still a part of Spain. Texas in 1823 was part of Mexico, which had just become independent from Spain in 1821. Benavides's father, José Jesus Benavides, and his uncle, Bacilio

Benavides, were officers in the Mexican army.

Benavides's youth was constantly interrupted by warfare. In 1836, when he was 13, Texas won its independence from Mexico in a brief war. However, Mexico and the new country of Texas could not decide where the new border between them should be. Benavides lived in the **disputed** border area between two large rivers, the Rio Grande and the Rio Nueces.

(continued)

SANTOS BENAVIDES

Many Latino families in this part of Texas wanted to be part of Mexico. However, they did not like a faraway government telling them what to do and taking their taxes. So, in 1838, a war started between the Mexican government in faraway Mexico City and the northern part of Mexico, where the Benavides family lived. This part of Mexico decided that it wanted to become independent just as Texas had two years earlier. Benavides participated bravely in this war, known as the Federalist War in Mexico.

Though Benavides was still a teenager, his job in this war was to lead 30 men in nighttime attacks against the Mexican government's soldiers. He and his men hid and waited for the government troops to march by. Then, when the troops came, the hidden attackers fired on them "under the cover of darkness." This was a very dangerous job, especially for a 15-year-old. But Benavides did it well. He gained a **reputation** as a good soldier. However, the Mexican government won the war. Many Mexican people were mad at the way the Mexican government had treated them in the war.

In the 1840's, Benavides started his own family and career. In 1842, he married Augustina Villareal. Over the years, they had four children together. Benavides also began to work in his uncle's business, trading with Mexican towns.

But, once again, war came to Laredo and interrupted Benavides's life. In 1845, Texas became a part of the United States. The United States said that Laredo and the disputed Texas land between the Rio Grande and the Rio Nueces was part of the United States. Troops arrived. Mexico attacked the troops, on the grounds that they were invading Mexican soil. As a result of this incident, a war between the United States and Mexico began in 1846. When it ended two years later, all the land north of the Rio Grande became a part of the United States, including Laredo. So, Benavides was now a citizen of the United States.

The biggest problem in the Laredo area in the **decade** before the Civil War was attacks by local Indians and **bandits**. Benavides earned respect in Laredo as a leader and soldier during wars against these two groups. Time and again in the 1850's, he was asked to lead a group in search of cattle thieves, murderers, or other criminals. The town was so happy with his successes that they elected Benavides mayor in 1857 and **chief justice** of the county in 1859.

Still, Benavides continued to fight to protect the town when needed. His most famous mission was in March 1861. This mission took place during the Indian wars against the local Comanche tribe. The Comanches, like most Native American tribes, had been living on their land for thousands of years. As one group after another—Spanish, Mexicans, Americans—took their land, some tribes fought back. The Comanches fought back by constantly attacking Laredo.

(continued)

SANTOS BENAVIDES

Benavides was put in charge of a small group that went in search of Comanches who were murdering resi- dents and stealing horses. He became a hero when he was able to capture these Comanches and get back nearly all of the 130 stolen horses. One month after further proving himself on this mission, the Civil War began.

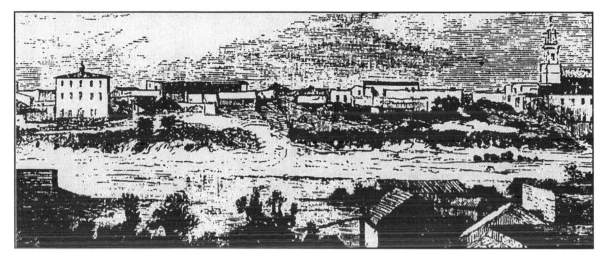

Laredo, Texas, in the mid-1800's

During the Civil War

Santos Benavides had become an important businessman in Laredo, Texas, when the state government voted to secede, or leave, the United States in February 1861. Most Anglo-Americans and Mexican-Americans in Texas sided with the Confederacy. Many Anglos in Texas were prejudiced against the *Tejanos*, as Mexican-Americans in Texas were called. So, Benavides wanted to show that *Tejanos* could fight in support of the Texas government as well as any Anglos could. Repeatedly throughout this long war, he succeeded in proving this.

In April 1861, Benavides recruited 68 men. He began to train them at Fort McIntosh, an **abandoned** fort near Laredo. Under the command of John "Rip" Ford, Benavides set out to fight against any threats along the Rio Grande. A rumor spread that another Latino named Juan Cortina was leading a Union Army near the town of Carrizo. Benavides led a force that drove Cortina out of this small Texas town on May 22, 1861. Ford commented on Benavides's "judgment, ability, and **gallantry**" in the battle. The governor of Texas was so happy with Benavides's bravery that he sent him a special **engraved** pistol as a thank-you gift. Both of these important Anglo Texans realized the role Benavides could play in the Civil War.

SANTOS BENAVIDES

In 1863, Benavides was promoted to major. He was put in charge of a larger company of *Tejano* soldiers. He then had continued success in another small battle. His new commander, General Bee, congratulated Benavides and his two brothers, who were also heroic Civil War leaders, in this way:

> *I especially recommend Major Benavides for his untiring energy and patriotism, and would respectfully suggest that the commanding general recognize officially the distinguished services of Major Benavides, and the firm, **unyielding** support which the companies of Laredo, commanded by Captains Refugio and Cristobal Benavides, all Mexicans, have ever given to our cause.*

The Union, however, was not happy with the Confederate success in south Texas. In November 1863, 7,000 Union soldiers invaded and took control of Brownsville, Texas, 200 miles down the Rio Grande from Laredo. The same month, Benavides was promoted to colonel and put in charge of his own regiment: The Benavides Regiment. This made him the highest-ranking Latino in the Confederacy. His new commander even promised to promote Benavides to brigadier general, but the war ended before this could happen.

The Benavides Regiment spent the winter months of 1863 to 1864 preparing for an attack by the Union army on the city of Laredo. By February 1864, Benavides was **exhausted** from three years of traveling around Texas—often without food, a bed, a tent, or a blanket. Finally, he **collapsed**. He was told by his doctor to stay in bed until he was better. However, the expected attack interrupted Benavides's recovery.

On March 19, 1864, a relative of the colonel, Cayetano de la Garza, rode his horse through downtown Laredo, yelling that 1,000 Union soldiers were **approaching** the town. This man later became known as the Paul Revere of Laredo. When Benavides heard the news, he jumped out of his sickbed and began organizing the defense of the town. He blamed his illness for the lack of preparation. He announced to his troops:

> *I have to fight to the last; though hardly able to stand, I shall die fighting. I won't retreat, no matter what force the [Union] has—I know I can depend on my boys.*

Expecting a large Union force, the Confederates **barricaded** the streets of Laredo and placed **snipers** on the rooftops. Benavides and 42 of his men took positions just outside of town and awaited the Union attack. It soon came. Three times that afternoon the Union attacked, and three times the Benavides forces pushed them back. Later, it was said that "Benavides and his men fought with the coolest bravery." The Union army quickly retreated back toward Brownsville and never again tried to attack Laredo. Benavides, despite his illness, continued to **pursue** them. After three days, he was so weakened that he fell off his horse and seriously injured

(continued)

SANTOS BENAVIDES

his head. A doctor ordered him to stay in bed and stop fighting until he became healthy. Unable to participate in the war directly, Benavides gave orders to his assistant from his sickbed. With these orders, the Benavides Regiment was finally able to push the Union army out of Brownsville, Texas, in July 1864.

During the next year, however, the war in the East gradually turned against the Confederates. Because of poor communication, many Texans did not hear about the end of the war and continued to fight. The **victorious** Union army finally caught up with Santos Benavides in July 1865. He was one of the last Confederate officers to surrender. He did so with **dignity** and honor.

After the Civil War

After the war ended, Santos Benavides turned his attention again to his career as a businessman. In late 1865, he saw a new business opportunity: protecting wagon trains passing through the dangerous postwar countryside of south Texas. Sometimes wagons were attacked 30 times during one trip through the region. For a fee of $1,000, Benavides and a number of his ex-soldiers helped wagons filled with goods and gold cross from town to town. As the area calmed down, he turned to other business opportunities, such as trade with towns in northern Mexico.

In 1879, Benavides returned to his other prewar career: politics. He became one of the few Latinos in the Texas state government when he was elected to the Texas **Legislature**. During the time he was serving as a legislator, Laredo grew into a major city and an important link to Mexico.

In 1883, a railroad was built to connect Laredo, Texas, and Saltillo, Mexico. Benavides was invited as an honored guest to the grand opening ceremony of the railroad station in Saltillo. As the first train from the United States pulled into the new station, Benavides spoke about the need for cooperation between Mexico and the United States. A reporter wrote that Benavides's **"benevolent** face beamed with happiness."

Benavides retired from the Texas Legislature in 1885. He died on April 23, 1891. That same year, an author of a book on successful Texans included this description of Santos Benavides:

> *Santos Benavides has been for more than half a century one of the best-known, most trusted, and **influential** citizens of southwest Texas. In peace or war, in joy or **sorrow**, he has **unflinchingly** done his duty to his fellow citizens, his family, his country, and his God. No man has ever done more.*

Though he lived in a different time and was not always on the side of justice, Santos Benavides was a true hero of the Civil War. He was also a Latino who succeeded in a field where few Latinos were allowed to succeed in the 1800's. For this Benavides is honored and remembered.

SANTOS BENAVIDES

GLOSSARY

disputed	argued about
reputation	general opinion held by people about another person
decade	a period of 10 years
bandits	robbers
chief justice	the head judge of a court
abandoned	deserted; given up completely
gallantry	heroic courage
engraved	cut or etched letters or designs
unyielding	not surrendering; not giving in
exhausted	completely tired out
collapsed	fell down
approaching	coming closer
barricaded	blocked with a barrier made quickly for defense
sniper	someone shooting from a hidden position
pursue	to follow in order to capture
victorious	having won a victory
dignity	self-respect
legislature	a lawmaking body
benevolent	kindly; good
beamed	shined brightly; smiled
influential	using one's power to affect others
sorrow	sadness
unflinchingly	firmly; without pausing

SANTOS BENAVIDES

Vocabulary Review

Word List

abandoned
approaching
bandits
barricaded
beamed
collapsed
decade
dignity
disputed
engraved
exhausted
gallantry
pursue
reputation
snipers
unyielding
victorious

Across

2. The car was _____ very fast.
8. The war started inside the _____ land.
10. The teacher had an _____ attitude about doing homework.
12. The sixties were a _____ of war and protest.
14. The _____ puppy sat sadly on the corner.
16. He won a trophy _____ with his name.
17. The _____ on the rooftops took aim at the kidnapper.

Down

1. After playing basketball for four hours, he was _____.
3. The building _____ in the earthquake.

4. The _____ robbed the train and then rode away.
5. The street was _____ so that no one could enter.
6. The police had to _____ the thief for two hours.
7. He had a _____ for being a good student.
9. He could not tell a lie because of his _____ .
11. Her softball team was _____ in the big game.
13. The firefighter said _____ was part of her job.
15. The proud mother's face _____ when her son won the award.

| SANTOS BENAVIDES | Understanding the Biography |

 ## Before the Civil War

1. In what year did Texas become independent from Mexico? _____

2. In what year did Texas become a part of the United States? _____

3. Describe the incident that led to a war between the United States and Mexico in 1846. _____

_____

_____

_____

4. Which of Benavides's experiences do you think helped to prepare him to be a hero in the Civil War? _____

_____

_____

During the Civil War

1. What did Benavides receive from the governor of Texas as a reward for his bravery? _____

2. Why was Benavides sick in bed when the attack on Laredo came?

_____

_____

SANTOS BENAVIDES

Understanding the Biography

3. Describe what Benavides did to organize the defense of Laredo on

   March 19, 1864: _____

   _____

   _____

4. If the government of Texas had voted to take the Union's side in the war, do you think Benavides would have fought with the Union?

   Explain. _____

   _____

   _____

★ After the Civil War

1. What was the first thing Benavides did when the war ended?

   _____

2. What political position did Benavides hold from 1879 to 1885?

   _____

3. An author wrote that Benavides had always "done his duty to his fellow citizens." List three times in his life when he helped his fellow

   citizens of Laredo. _____

   _____

   _____

4. Which of these times in his life do you think Benavides showed the

   most heroism? Explain why you chose that event. _____

   _____

SANTOS BENAVIDES

Creative Project:
Writing a News Article

Santos Benavides's heroic defense of Laredo was the subject of many newspaper articles. Pretend that you are a reporter on the scene of the Battle of Laredo. First, take notes about the battle on the notepad page below.

The Battle of Laredo

Who: _____

What: _____

When: _____

What happened: _____

_____

_____

_____

Why it happened: _____

_____

_____

Now, use your notes to write the newspaper article on the following page. Include a headline at the top. Draw a picture in the box to the right.

SANTOS BENAVIDES

Creative Project:
Writing a News Article

The Laredo Times

_____

_____ _____
_____ _____
_____ _____
_____ _____
_____ _____
_____ _____
_____
_____
_____
_____
_____
_____
_____
_____
_____
_____

Name _____

Date _____

SANTOS BENAVIDES

Map Activity: The Civil War in Southeastern Texas

This map shows major Civil War battles in southeast Texas, where Santos Benavides lived and fought. Use it to answer the questions below.

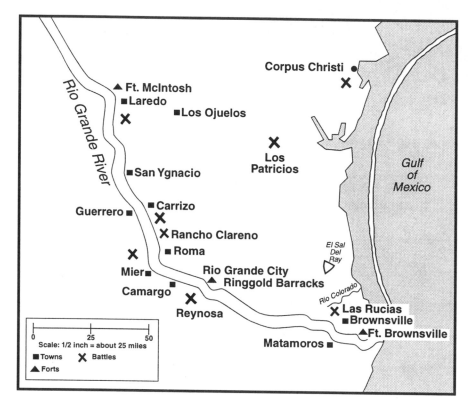

1. Color the Rio Grande blue. Label the area south of the river "Mexico" and the area north of the river "Texas."

2. Which battles took place in Mexican territory? _____

_____

3. Find Carrizo, the first town Benavides helped defend in the Civil War. Use the map scale (1 inch: about 25 miles) to estimate the approximate distance Benavides traveled from Laredo to Carrizo: _____ miles

4. The Union troops moved north from Brownsville to attack Laredo. Draw a line to show their route to Laredo. Then draw the line heading back to Brownsville after Benavides defeated them in The Battle of Laredo. How far did the Union troops travel? _____ miles

60   *Latino Heroes of the Civil War*

RAFAEL CHACÓN

Union Hero of the Battle of Valverde, Westernmost Battle of the Civil War

Rafael Chacón in his uniform during the Civil War

*Rafael Chacón's 92-year life was full of adventure and danger. He joined the army at the age of 11, and found himself involved in a series of wars in the wild New Mexican territory for the next 20 years. Chacón then became a successful legislator, rancher, and sheriff in a famous old western town. Finally, he spent his later years writing his **memoirs**. These memoirs provide a rare look at the perspectives of Latinos on the Civil War in the southwestern United States.*

Before the Civil War

Rafael Chacón was born in the city of Santa Fe, New Mexico, on April 22,

1833. At the time of his birth, New Mexico was a long-ignored northern part of Mexico, which had only recently become independent from Spain. Two of his ancestors had served as governors of New Mexico when it was considered part of New Spain. His father, Don Albino Chacón, held many important government positions in New Mexico. His grandfather, Don Felipe, was a wealthy and respected rancher and businessman. From these ancestors young Chacón learned that honor was the most important thing a person could have.

In 1844, at the age of 11, Chacón became a cadet at a military school in Chihuahua, Mexico. Because he was the youngest cadet at the school, he was often taken advantage of by some of the older boys. They would ask to borrow his money, horse, and clothing, but never repaid him or returned what they took. Young Chacón refused to allow this to interfere with his studies. Instead, he continued with his academics and military training, while **cleverly** hiding his money in a belt under his shirt.

In late 1845, Chacón had his first military experience. A war broke out that year between the United States and Mexico. During this war, which was known in the United States as the Mexican War, the United States sent a large army to invade New Mexico. New Mexico was a part of Mexico that the U.S. government wanted to take over. Chacón's father asked to excuse his son because of his young age, but this request was refused. So, the 13-year-old

(continued)

RAFAEL CHACÓN

was put in charge of a piece of light **artillery** and sent to meet the invaders. Luckily, Chacón never had to fight, because the New Mexican commander decided the American force was too strong. He ordered his troops back to Santa Fe, their capital. The United States won the war in 1848 and took over New Mexico. Chacón's father, who had been a powerful leader in Santa Fe when it was part of Mexico, refused to work with the Americans. Instead, he chose to move his family to the northern mountains.

Chacón worked in various occupations for the next decade. He was a laborer, a trader, and a buffalo hunter. But, he began to earn his reputation for bravery during the Indian Wars of the 1850's. In 1855, a war broke out between an Indian tribe called the Utes and the New Mexican settlers. Both Anglo-American and Mexican-American settlers went in search of the Utes. Chacón joined the army of settlers. He suffered through the **bitter** winter snowstorms with thin clothes and a single blanket without complaining. Walking through deep snow, he would "be unable to breathe from cold, fatigue, and being soaked." Yet, he continued, anxious to prove his bravery in battle. At one point, when he thought a **mounted** officer was trying to stay in the rear to avoid combat, Chacón said to him, "Let me have that horse to follow the enemy, you **coward**." Chacón then traded his mule for the scared officer's horse and

rode to the front of the battle, where he fought with courage.

After a peace treaty ended the conflict, Chacón turned his attention to the trading business. Throughout the late 1850's, he led trading expeditions into the Indian territories, and later into northern Mexico. In 1858, he moved to Santa Fe and built a house with the money he had earned from trading. Chacón started to set up a business shipping goods to Kansas City, but events in the East forced him to change his plans.

During the Civil War

Soon after the Civil War broke out in April 1861, there were **rumors** that the Confederates in Texas might try to invade New Mexico. The Confederates planned to invade New Mexico on their way to the valuable gold mines of Colorado and California. The Union army began recruiting any Anglo or Latino men in the region who might be able to lead soldiers in the defense of New Mexico. Because of his reputation as a courageous and skilled fighter, Rafael Chacón was immediately made a captain when he joined the Union army on August 13, 1861. Though just 28 years old, he was put in charge of a Spanish-speaking regiment of Latino volunteers —Company K. His commander was a famous **frontiersman** named Kit Carson.

Chacón was very protective of his men. Once, when an officer under his command was insulting his Mexican soldiers, he dismissed the officer from Company K. He was also **strict** with his

(continued)

RAFAEL CHACÓN

soldiers when necessary. He earned the respect of Union commanders like Kit Carson, who spoke Spanish. But, because Chacón did not speak English well enough to communicate with many of the other Union officers, he was often treated badly by them. Once they tried to take his men's horses away to be used by a company of English-speaking soldiers. Chacón had a bilingual friend write several letters to convince the Union officers to not take the horses. His men were the only Spanish-speaking soldiers allowed to keep their horses.

While awaiting the invasion from the Confederate Texans, Chacón's men were sent to Albuquerque, New Mexico, to serve as local police. They captured a group of murderers on a dangerous night mission into the mountains. Later, they went in search of a group of horse thieves. As Chacón entered a dark house where the thieves were hiding, someone put a rifle to his chest and fired. Luckily, Chacón was able to twist his body so that the bullet merely burned his shirt.

On February 16, 1862, after six months of waiting, 3,000 Confederate Texan troops under the command of General Henry Sibley were spotted near the Union fort. Chacón and his men twice rode their horses in front of the Union troops to try to scare them. Several shots were fired, but the Confederates **retreated**. These were the first shots of the Civil War in New Mexico.

For the next few days, Chacón and his troops were ordered to occupy a **mesa**—a high, flat area—and prevent the enemy from taking it. Cannonballs fell near the mesa, sending rocks flying toward Chacón's soldiers. They held their ground, even though two soldiers were injured by the rocks.

Finally, on February 21, the main battle began in a wooded valley in an area just east of the Rio Grande called Valverde. This became known as the Battle of Valverde. Chacón's mounted company was one of the first to arrive. In the early morning, each side lined up on opposite sides of the woods and began shooting cannonballs at each other. At 1:00 P.M., a piece of Texas artillery began bombing the position where Chacón's company was waiting. After constant bombardment, Chacón decided to attack the position where the artillery was located. The Confederates were so surprised by this that they ran away and left the cannon behind. Chacón successfully captured the Texas artillery piece.

At 4:00, all of Carson's New Mexican Volunteers, including Chacón's company, charged at the Confederates. Chacón described the attack as follows:

*We made the attack full of courage and almost in a **frenzy**. First checking and then driving the enemy back through blood and fire, we forced them to flee to the hills.*

Chacón's successful attack had put his company deep inside enemy territory. He thought they had won the battle. Unfortunately, while Chacón's men were fighting heroically and winning, the other troops were overrun

(continued)

RAFAEL CHACÓN

by a Confederate force of 1,000 men who had hidden in the woods behind a hill. When finally ordered to retreat, Chacón's company was the last part of the Union army to cross the river to safety. Thus, in the historic Battle of Valverde—the first in New Mexico, and the westernmost battle of the entire Civil War—Rafael Chacón was a true hero. He was involved in several parts of this key battle and fought bravely in each instance.

Though the Confederates had won the Battle of Valverde, they were badly weakened by Chacón and others. They had hundreds of **casualties**. This weakened invasion force headed north to Santa Fe, towards the Colorado gold mines, only to be defeated just one month later at the Battle of Glorieta Pass (see Manuel Chaves). Throughout April 1862, the Confederates made their long retreat back to Texas.

Chacón was sent on a mission to make sure that all the Confederates left New Mexico. On the night of April 15, Chacón and a few of his men got lost in the woods while searching for one of the Confederate groups. They decided to hide until the morning. When the sun rose, a Confederate guard spotted them and fired at them. Chacón fired back, and the Confederates fled into the forest. As Chacón later wrote:

> I had the honor to exchange the first shots with the enemy Confederates at the beginning of the campaign on February 16 at Fort Craig. Now, I also had the honor to [fire] the last shots on the enemy at the end of the Texan invasion.

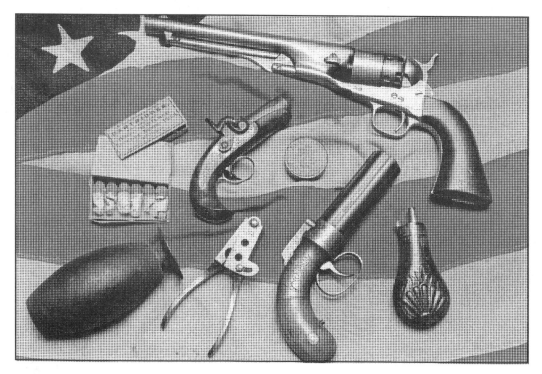

The tools of the Civil War—both in the East and the West

(continued)

RAFAEL CHACÓN

After the battles of 1862, the war never returned to the Southwest. The Confederates gave up their plans to capture the gold mines of Colorado and California, thanks to the heroism of men like Rafael Chacón. Having helped drive these invaders from his land, Chacón was now given other duties as a Union officer. In the winter of 1862, he was sent to build a fort in the windy northern mountains. Chacón completed this task; then, in 1863, he was asked to go on a historic mission—an expedition to the newly created territory of Arizona. The new governor of Arizona, John I. Goodwin, commented in a report of the journey:

> My **acquaintance** with Captain Chacón only increased the high estimate I had formed of his abilities as a soldier. He is well acquainted with the Indian mode of warfare, and is extremely **cool**.

The journey home from Arizona was very difficult. At times, Chacón and his men had to march through three feet of snow. Also, Chacón was suffering from rheumatism, a disease that makes your joints ache. Exhausted, he returned to New Mexico in 1864. There, he received the news that he had been promoted to major. Shortly afterwards, he was made the commander of Fort Stanton. He participated in numerous campaigns against the Navajos, a tribe that had been attacking the New Mexicans. Though he fought hard against the Navajos and other Indians, Chacón always insisted that they be treated well when the fighting was over. When the Union army wanted to move the Navajos to a desert area with bad water, he wrote an angry letter to the army, demanding that they change the location.

On September 2, 1864, Chacón was honorably **discharged** from the U.S. Army and returned to Santa Fe.

After the Civil War

After the war ended, Chacón was so popular that he became involved briefly in politics. From 1865 to 1866, he served as a senator in the New Mexico Territorial Legislature. Then, in 1867, he became secretary of the legislature. Chacón was perhaps too honest for politics. He wrote that "honor and dignity were sold and respectability forgotten."

In 1870, Chacón decided to move north to the territory of Colorado. He settled with his family in a town called Trinidad. This was a classic old western town. Famous western gunfighters like Doc Holiday, Wyatt Earp, and Billy the Kid all spent time in the town. Chacón was one of the town's first settlers to see the potential for raising sheep and cattle on the open, grassy lands around the town. He became **wealthy**, but his generosity often left him broke. In 1885, he became the town's sheriff.

Throughout the rest of his life, Chacón was sought out by local historians who were interested in his long and eventful life. In 1906, he began writing his memoirs—the story of his life. He finished the autobiography in 1912, but it was not published until 1987.

(continued)

RAFAEL CHACÓN

Chacón died on July 23, 1925, at the age of 92. Throughout his long and interesting life, he always believed in three things: religion, education, and honor. He gave so much of his income to the local church that a hospital was named after him. He pushed his children to do well in school, and they did. One of his sons graduated from Notre Dame University in Indiana and became a successful bilingual lawyer. But, it was honor that was most important for Rafael Chacón. Near the end of his life, when he had given away most of the money he had earned, he wrote, "I am poor, and my only **inheritance** is my honor." For that, along with his many accomplishments, he is remembered as a great hero.

GLOSSARY

memoirs	a biography or writing of events from personal knowledge
cadet	student in training to be a military officer
cleverly	intelligently done
artillery	cannons or other large mounted guns
bitter	harsh; painful
mounted	serving on horseback
coward	one easily scared; not brave
rumors	stories that may or may not be true
reputation	general opinion held by people about another
frontiersman	one living in an area between settled and unsettled lands
strict	closely and carefully enforcing rules
retreated	withdrew or pulled back during an attack
mesa	high, flat land with steep sides
frenzy	wild excitement
casualty	soldier who is killed or wounded
acquaintance	knowledge of a person or thing
cool	calm and brave
discharged	released or let go from the military
wealthy	rich
inheritance	something received from a parent or ancestor after death

RAFAEL CHACÓN

Vocabulary Review

Word List

artillery
bitter
cadet
casualty
cleverly
coward
frenzy
frontiersman
memoirs
mesa
mounted
reputation
retreated
rumors
strict
wealthy

Across

3. Many presidents write their _____ after leaving office.
5. Our _____ was too powerful for the enemy.
10. The _____ had to live at a military school far away from home.
11. If you are friendly to others, you will probably have a good _____.
12. Karla _____ solved the computer problem.
13. The sharks ate the fish in a _____.
14. That teacher is so _____ we can't get away with anything.
15. The _____ cowboys did tricks in the rodeo.

Down

1. The _____ ran away when he saw the bee.
2. I could see the whole valley from on top of the _____.
4. The _____ wind hit her face, but she kept walking.
6. The doctor was not only _____ but wise.
7. The mean girl liked to spread false _____ about other students.
8. Davy Crockett was a famous _____.
9. The soldier was the first _____ in the long battle.
11. The soldiers _____ when they realized they could not win the battle.

RAFAEL CHACÓN

Understanding the Biography

Before the Civil War

1. What did Chacón learn from his ancestors? _____

_____

2. What did young Chacón do to stop older cadets from stealing his

   money? _____

_____

3. How was 13-year-old Chacón able to avoid fighting in the Mexican

   War? _____

_____

4. Describe how Chacón showed his bravery in the 1855 war against the

   Utes: _____

_____

_____

During the Civil War

1. Who was Chacón's first Civil War commander? _____

2. What did Chacón do when some officers wanted to take away his

   men's horses? _____

_____

_____

(continued)

| RAFAEL CHACÓN | **Understanding the Biography** |

3. Describe Chacón's brave actions during the Battle of Valverde:

_____

_____

_____

4. How do you think Chacón felt when he was told to retreat?

_____

_____

★ After the Civil War

1. How did Chacón become wealthy later in life? _____

_____

2. What three things did Chacón believe in throughout life? _____

_____

3. As sheriff of Trinidad, what do you think Chacón would have done if

a gunfighter tried to cause trouble? _____

_____

_____

4. What do you think he meant by, "I am poor and my only inheritance

is my honor"? _____

_____

_____

RAFAEL CHACÓN

Creative Project: Designing a Poster

At the beginning of the Civil War in New Mexico, the Union army recruited Latinos throughout the territory. The army had to convince the Latinos to give up their jobs in cities or on farms, leave their families, and join an army that had defeated them when they were part of Mexico 15 years earlier. Furthermore, they had to face prejudice, the possibility of not being paid or clothed for many months, and, of course, the risk of battle.

Design a poster that urges Latinos in New Mexico to join your army despite all of these reasons not to join. First, make a rough sketch of your poster below. Then, have someone edit your writing before making the final poster on the following page.

Join the Union Army!

(continued)

**Creative Project:
Designing a Poster**

RAFAEL CHACÓN

CIVIL WAR RECRUITMENT POSTER

 Join the Union Army!

Name _____

Date _____

RAFAEL CHACÓN

Map Activity:
The Battle of Valverde

This is an actual sketch drawn by Rafael Chacón. It shows the Union and Confederate positions at the beginning of the Battle of Valverde. The map was included in his memoirs. Imagine that Chacón needs you to translate it into English and label it as described below. Then, his English-speaking Union army commanders will fully understand his heroism in the battle.

1. Write the English words next to the Spanish words in the map key.

2. Try to translate the short paragraph on the lines above the key.

3. Translate and label the four cardinal directions on the map compass.

4. Label the river "Rio Grande" and color it blue.

5. Chacón and the New Mexico Volunteers were the second cavalry unit moving up from the south. Label the unit; then draw an arrow showing them attacking the Confederates. Put a "1" on the arrow.

6. Draw an arrow showing the hidden Confederate infantry and cavalry attacking the Union artillery. Put a "2" on this arrow.

7. Draw arrows showing the other Union soldiers retreating across the river. Put a "3" on this arrow.

8. Draw an arrow showing Chacón's company retreating last. Put a "4" on this arrow.

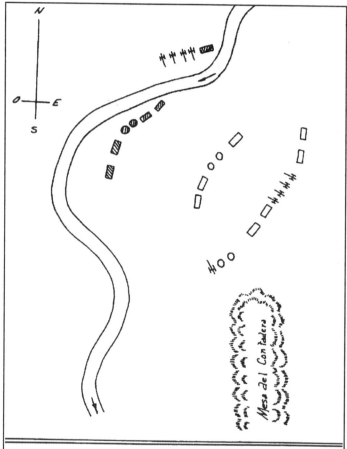

MANUEL CHAVES

Union Hero of the Battle of Glorieta Pass, The Gettysburg of the West

Manuel Chaves

Manuel Chaves lived an eventful life in the wild American West of the 1800's. In fact, he was personally involved in almost every key event of that period, including three major wars: the Mexican-American War, the Indian Wars, and the Civil War. In each war, Chaves earned such a great reputation as a courageous and fierce fighter that he became known to fellow residents of New Mexico as El Lioncito—the Little Lion.

Before the Civil War

Manuel Chaves was born into an important New Mexican family on October 18, 1818. His earliest ancestors were Spanish soldiers who were among the first to explore Central and South America. His later ancestors helped found the Spanish (and then Mexican) territory of New Mexico and its capital, Santa Fe. His father, Julián Chaves, was a successful rancher and farmer outside the town of Albuquerque. His mother, María Luz García, had moved to New Mexico from the town of Zacatecas, Mexico.

In 1827, when Manuel Chaves was nine years old, his family moved to a bigger ranch in the **frontier** town of Cebolleta. This was a dangerous place for settlers. The local Navajo and Apache tribes were not happy to see the land they had occupied for thousands of years being taken by these foreigners from Spain. Some Spanish settlers made matters worse by making it a practice to kidnap and **enslave** Indian children. In response, the tribes repeatedly attacked frontier towns such as Cebolleta.

When Chaves was about 15 years old, he was involved in his first—and almost his last—major battle. He and his two brothers and a dozen other teenagers from Cebolleta went on a trip in the mountains, deep inside Navajo territory. Two hundred miles away from home, the group was attacked by Navajos. Only Chaves and a younger brother survived the battle. The older brother and all the

(continued)

MANUEL CHAVES

others were killed in the attack. The two survivors, however, were both seriously wounded, and they had to walk back home alone through Navajo territory. After walking for two days, they finally lay down to rest. When Chaves awoke, his younger brother had died from his injuries. Despite the pain and grief, Chaves pushed himself the last miles and made it home safely.

Hearing of the attack, another brother wanted to get **revenge** by killing some local Navajos who had not been involved in the battle. But, according to legend, Chaves left his sickbed and talked his angry brother out of killing the innocent Navajos. Thus, even as a youth, Chaves showed two traits that would stay with him for the rest of his life: courage and fairness. These traits are the mark of a true hero.

A couple of years after recovering from this incident, Chaves had his first official military experience. At this time, New Mexico was a northern state in the newly independent country of Mexico. New Mexico was far away from most of the big cities in southern Mexico and had few Mexican soldiers to defend it. So, sometimes a group of settlers would try to **overthrow** the government in Santa Fe, New Mexico's capital. When this happened in 1837, Chaves joined the Mexican army and helped the Mexican government recover control of Santa Fe.

Chaves left Santa Fe in 1839, after a dispute with the governor of New Mexico. At age 21, he traveled to St. Louis, Missouri. There, he started a successful fruit business. Unfortunately for Chaves, the man he started the business with disappeared one day in 1840, with all the store's money. In an attempt to recover the money, Chaves followed the man to New York and then to Havana, Cuba. But he never found him.

Despite the bad luck with his business, Chaves's time in St. Louis was valuable in another way. He had the opportunity to learn a new language: English. In New Mexico, almost everyone spoke Spanish. As Chaves traveled around buying fruit for his business, he became bilingual. This enabled him to trade with more customers and helped him later when he returned to Santa Fe in 1841. With more and more English-speaking settlers moving to Texas and New Mexico, there was a need for **interpreters**. So, Chaves joined the Mexican army as a secretary and interpreter. In 1844, with his new career secure, he married María Vicenta Labadie and started a family.

Chaves's quiet family life ended in 1846, when war broke out between the United States and Mexico. During this war, which became known in the United States as The Mexican War, the U.S. Army headed toward Santa Fe to attack. Chaves and others told the Mexican governor to stand and fight to defend Mexican territory. Instead, the governor fled south with most of the army.

Chaves was arrested as the U.S. Army conquered Santa Fe and the rest of New Mexico. At Chaves's trial for **treason**, his lawyer argued that Chaves could

(continued)

MANUEL CHAVES

not be considered a traitor because he was a citizen of Mexico, not the United States. Therefore, Chaves was actually defending his country and deserved "the admiration of all brave men." Chaves was found innocent and released.

Later, when he saw that the U.S. Army was treating his people with respect, he joined the Americans and fought bravely at the Battle of Taos. At one point, he saved his commander from death.

Throughout the 1850's, Chaves tried to retire from fighting to work on a sheep ranch that he had started, but events prevented him from working in peace. Because of his knowledge of the

mountains and his abilities as a soldier, he was asked to participate in the wars between settlers and Indians. He served as a captain in the U.S. Army and was recognized for his bravery in these bloody wars. More important, the lessons he learned in these mountain battles served him well later, when the Civil War broke out.

During the Civil War

When the Civil War started in April 1861, many U.S. Army commanders in New Mexico resigned and joined the Confederacy. One of these officers tried to get Chaves to join him by offering him a colonel's rank. Chaves, however, had just signed an **oath** promising to defend the Union. So, he responded:

I Manuel Chaves Lieutenant Colonel, of the 2ᵈ Regiment of N M Volunteers do solemnly swear that I will bear true faith and allegiance to the United States of America, and that I will serve them honestly and faithfully against all their enemies and opposers whatsoever; and observe and obey the orders of the President of the United States, and the orders of the officers appointed over me, according to the Rules and Articles for the government of the Armies of the United States.

Sworn and subscribed to this *1st* day of *August, a. D., 1861,* before me

C B Clark
Nort. Public

Manuel Chaves
Teniente Coronel del 2ᵈ Reg.ᵗᵒ de Volunt.ˢ de N. ʲᶜᵒ.

Manuel Chaves had to sign this oath of allegiance to prove his loyalty to the United States at the beginning of the Civil War. Many other officers resigned and joined the Confederacy.

(continued)

MANUEL CHAVES

Colonel, when I took the oath of allegiance to the United States, I swore to protect the American flag, and if my services are needed I shall give them to the country of my adoption and her flag.

The Union army remembered Chaves for his bravery and skills. They put him in charge of Fort Fauntleroy and promoted him to lieutenant colonel. He was in charge of a large group called The First New Mexico Volunteers. These volunteers were mostly poor Latinos who had recently become U.S. citizens. They fought bravely, despite their lack of training—and having to face racist attitudes of some in the non-Latino U.S. officers.

The volunteers had their first opportunity to fight when the Civil War came to New Mexico in February 1862. The Confederate army wanted to conquer New Mexico because it was the **gateway** to the goldfields of California and Colorado. If the Confederates could capture New Mexico, they would be able to get the gold from these other places more easily. With this gold, the South would be better able to pay for all the supplies and weapons they would need to fight the richer North. So, they sent an army from Texas, led by the experienced officer General Sibley, to invade New Mexico.

The first battle was fought in a field near the town of Valverde. (See Rafael Chacón page 61.) Chaves and his men

lost the battle. But Chaves's commander wrote that Chaves himself had fought with "**zeal** and energy."

Sibley's men then headed north toward Fort Union, near Santa Fe. Chaves and the remaining New Mexico Volunteers took another route north to try to defend the fort. In mid-March, they met up with a group of Colorado volunteers led by Major John Chivington. By this time, Sibley's men were inside Santa Fe. They were planning an attack on Fort Union, the main Union fort between Santa Fe and the goldfields of Colorado.

Chaves took six soldiers and went on a spy mission to Santa Fe to find out how he would attack. Chaves's spy group learned that Sibley was going to head the next day along the Santa Fe Trail, through an area known as Glorieta Pass, toward Fort Union. With this important information provided by Chaves, Chivington made a plan which led to the most important Civil War battle in New Mexico—the Battle of Glorieta Pass.

On March 26, Major Chivington sent half of his army to attack directly, while he led his troops to surround them at the pass. In order to get there on time, however, he needed someone who was familiar with the forest trails. Who better than Manuel Chaves—a skilled and experienced mountain man and soldier?

Studying the mountain **terrain** while Chivington searched for the best route on old maps, Chaves finally said that he would bet his life that they would arrive at Glorieta Pass by heading straight west. On March 28, Chaves

(continued)

MANUEL CHAVES

Manuel Chaves guided Union troops on a surprise attack down this cliff above Glorieta Pass.
The daring attack helped stop the Confederacy's western push and drove the invaders back to Texas.

carefully led the army through 16 miles of mountain wilderness. They ended up on a 200-foot **cliff** above the pass. Chaves stopped there and said, "You are right on top of them, Major Chivington." They were indeed. But rather than being above the enemy army, they had discovered a greater prize: the enemy's base camp. Right below them were more than 75 wagons, 500 horses, and all the other supplies that Sibley would need to keep his army going on to the goldfields of Colorado and California. Destruction of this hidden base camp was the key to defeating the Texans.

Chaves chose the best route down the high, **steep** cliff. The group of Union soldiers started quietly climbing down. It was so difficult that they had to use ropes and leather straps. One man hit a rock, and suddenly the Texans realized they were being surprised. They started firing a cannon at the cliff. But the Union soldiers were able to make it down safely. After a short battle, they took control of the camp and destroyed all of the horses and supplies. When the Confederates heard about this event, they pleaded for an end to the fighting. Then they retreated back to Texas.

This **daring** attack—made possible by Manuel Chaves—had broken the back of the Confederate invaders from Texas. They never again tried to invade New Mexico. Because of its significance, the Battle of Glorieta Pass later became known as The Gettysburg of the West.

(continued)

MANUEL CHAVES

After the Civil War

With the threat from the Confederacy over, Chaves wanted to return to his peaceful life as a sheep rancher in northern New Mexico. But, when he got home, he found out that local Navajos had taken 30,000 of his sheep. With settlers taking more and more of the Navajo's best farmland, they had responded by taking this ready source of food: the settlers' **livestock**.

Chaves decided to pursue the Navajos to get his sheep back. Not only was he unsuccessful in recovering the sheep, but he ended up walking into the worst battle of his life. His small band of 15 settlers was attacked by the Navajos. After an all-day battle, only Chaves and two others survived. Luckily, all Chaves had to show for this were two bullet holes through his hat.

During the 1870's and 1880's, Chaves and a brother, Don Román, acquired and built up other lands next to his ranch. They expanded their livestock business. Despite his age and poor health, Chaves couldn't resist riding his horse around the ranch supervising his workers. In 1885, he was seriously injured when an ox tossed him to the ground. Still, he kept on working.

In the late 1880's, a journalist named Charles Lummis visited the **elderly** Chaves after hearing tales of the heroism of the man known as *El Lioncito*. Later, Lummis wrote a biography in which he described Chaves as "a courtly Spanish gentleman, brave as a lion, **tender** as a woman, spotless of honor, and **modest** as heroic."

Chaves died in January 1889. His son, Amador, became a hero in other fields. As New Mexico's superintendent of public schools, he brought schools to isolated villages so that everyone would have an opportunity to be educated. Later, he became mayor of Santa Fe. His father would have been proud of him.

MANUEL CHAVES

GLOSSARY

fierce	wild and passionate
frontier	area between settled and unsettled land
enslave	to make a slave
revenge	to get back at someone in response to something done to you
overthrow	to conquer a government or leader
interpreters	people who explain or translate a language
treason	helping the enemy of one's country
traitor	one who helps the enemy of one's country
oath	a promise in God's name
gateway	means of entry or exit
zeal	enthusiasm for a cause
terrain	a stretch of land and its features
cliff	high, steep rock or mountains
steep	having a sharp rise or slope
daring	brave and adventurous
livestock	domestic farm animals such as horses, sheep, and cattle
elderly	somewhat old
tender	light, gentle
modest	not wanting to talk of one's accomplishments

Name _____

Date _____

MANUEL CHAVES

Vocabulary Review

Word List

cliff
daring
elderly
enslave
fierce
frontier
gateway
interpreters
livestock
modest
oath
overthrow
pursue
revenge
steep
tender
terrain
traitor
treason
zeal

Across

1. The _____ woman told many stories about her life.
3. The _____ student did not tell every one about his A.
5. The cat wanted to _____ the mouse, but the little creature went into the wall.
6. You must take an _____ of allegiance to become a citizen.
9. Ellis Island in New York was the _____ to the United States for many immigrants.
11. Be careful climbing the _____.
13. The _____ tiger attacked quickly and angrily.
14. A soldier can be killed for _____ during a war.
15. The people tried to _____ the mean king.
17. To _____ is to not let someone be free.
18. The mother sings a _____ song to her baby.

19. The trip to the moon was exciting and _____.

Down

2. The farmer told his son to take care of the _____.
4. The rocky _____ was difficult to cross.
7. The _____ told the enemy the secret code.
8. It was hard to climb the pyramid because the sides were so _____.
10. His _____ helped the soldier to keep fighting even when tired.
12. The company needed many _____ to help sell its products to other countries.
13. As the East became crowded, more people moved to the western _____.
16. Many people get in trouble when they try to get _____ for something done to them.

Latino Heroes of the Civil War

MANUEL CHAVES

Understanding the Biography

 ## Before the Civil War

1. What did Chaves's earliest ancestors do? _____

_____

2. How did Chaves learn English? _____

_____

3. What did Chaves do during his teen years that showed his courage

and fairness? _____

_____

_____

4. If Chaves were alive today, what different jobs might he get with his

excellent bilingual skills? _____

_____

_____

 ## During the Civil War

1. What was Chaves's first job in the Union army?_____

_____

2. What did Chaves learn on his spy mission to Santa Fe? _____

_____

_____

(continued)

| MANUEL CHAVES |

Understanding the Biography

3. Why did the Confederate Texans want to conquer New Mexico?

_____

_____

4. What do you think would have happened in the Civil War if the Confederates had won the Battle of Glorieta Pass?

_____

_____

_____

_____

★ After the Civil War

1. What did Chaves want to do when the Civil War in New Mexico

   ended? _____

   _____

2. Who visited Chaves and wrote the first biography of him? _____

   _____

3. Why was Chaves known as *El Lioncito*? _____

   _____

4. At which event in his life do you think Chaves showed the most

   heroism? Explain why you chose that event. _____

   _____

   _____

MANUEL CHAVES

Creative Project: Writing a Letter

Manuel Chaves was deeply involved in the Battle of Glorieta Pass. Pretend that you are Chaves. You want to write a letter to your friend and fellow New Mexican soldier Rafael Chacón. In the letter, tell Chacón all about your role in this exciting battle. Follow the writing process steps. (See Loreta Velázquez activity, page 30.)

Brainstorm

Look in the section titled During the Civil War (page 75). List the different things that Chaves did that led to a victory in the Battle of Glorieta Pass.

1. _____

2. _____

3. _____

4. _____

5. _____

First Draft   Now, take these details and use them to write the letter on the following page.

Revise and Edit   Next, have someone read your letter and give you suggestions on how to make it better.

Rewrite   Then, rewrite the paragraph using the suggestions.

Proofread   Now, have someone check the paragraph once again to make sure there are no mistakes.

Final Copy   Finally, rewrite the paragraph again very neatly, or use a typewriter or computer.

(continued)

MANUEL CHAVES

Creative Project: Writing a Letter

March 28, 1862

Dear Rafael,

_____

_____

_____

_____

_____

_____

_____

_____

_____

_____

_____

_____

_____

_____

_____

_____

_____

Your friend,

Manuel

MANUEL CHAVES

Map Activity:
New Mexico in the Civil War

This activity involves a battle map of New Mexico and surrounding states. Manuel Chaves spent most of his life this area. Use the map on the next page to answer these questions:

1. What four U.S. states surround New Mexico? _____

_____

What Mexican state is to the south of New Mexico? _____

Lightly shade each state with a colored pencil or crayon. Do not color New Mexico.

2. What major river runs north through the center of New Mexico?

_____ Color this river blue.

Trace the Confederate invaders' route from El Paso, Texas, to Glorieta Pass. Why do you think they traveled alongside the Rio Grande?

_____

_____

3. Find Valverde, the site of the Battle of Valverde, and Fort Union. Manuel Chaves fought at Valverde and then traveled north to Fort Union. Use the map scale to estimate the distance he and his men

traveled: _____

4. Locate Santa Fe, where Chaves went to spy on the Confederate soldiers. Then, locate Fort Union, where the Confederates wanted to attack. Why did they choose to travel south through Glorieta Pass

instead of heading directly northeast to Fort Union? _____

_____

(*Hint:* Find the physical feature that stood in their way.)

(continued)

Name _____

Date _____

MANUEL CHAVES

Map Activity:
New Mexico in the Civil War

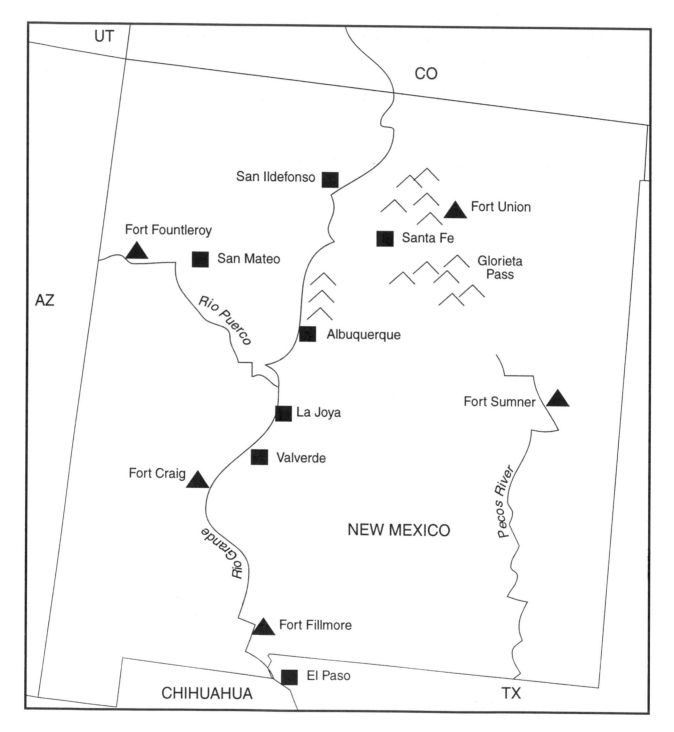

UT

CO

San Ildefonso ■

▲ Fort Union

Fort Fountleroy
▲

■ San Mateo

■ Santa Fe

AZ

Rio Puerco

Glorieta
Pass

■ Albuquerque

Fort Sumner ▲

■ La Joya

■ Valverde

NEW MEXICO

Fort Craig ▲

Pecos River

Rio Grande

▲ Fort Fillmore

■ El Paso

CHIHUAHUA

TX

Teacher Guide

Answer Key

David Farragut

Vocabulary Review

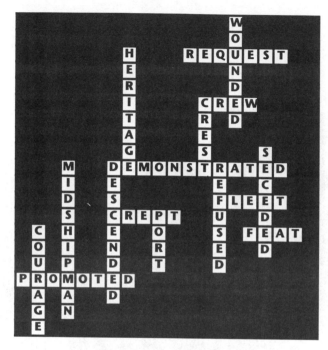

Understanding the Biography

Before the Civil War

1. Don Pedro Ferragut, Jorge Farragut
2. midshipman
3. He warned the captain (his stepfather) about prisoners who were going to attack. He bravely commanded a ship and stood up to a British captain. He saved a sailor from being killed by a cannonball.
4. Answers may vary.

During the Civil War

1. New Orleans, Mobile (Mobile Bay)
2. Abraham Lincoln
3. Both battles involved heavily defended ports. Farragut ran his ships through heavy fire and explosions. The Union won each battle, and Farragut was promoted after each.
4. scared, nervous; relieved, happy

After the Civil War

1. 69 years old
2. He investigated his family history and added his life to the family crest.
3. He became the first full admiral in U.S. history.
4. Answers may vary.

Map Activity: Farragut's Naval Battles

1. Color the rivers and gulf on the map.
2. Color each of the seven states on the map.
3. Fort Jackson and Fort St. Philip.
4. April 29, 1862
5. Port Hudson; July 9, 1863
6. August 5, 1864
7. Draw an arrow on the map.
8. The river was not deep enough for his ships.

Loreta Vélazquez

Vocabulary Review

Understanding the Biography

Before the Civil War

1. sent Cortés to Mexico in 1510
2. Joan of Arc
3. She wanted to become a soldier and fight as well as any man for a great cause.
4. Answers will vary.

During the Civil War

1. Bull Run, Ball's Bluff, Fort Donaldson, and Shiloh
2. She worked as a spy.
3. First, she had a tailor make a special uniform. Then, she had a barber give her a man's style haircut. Next, a friend helped her glue on a false mustache and practice disguising her voice and mannerisms. Finally, she changed her name.
4. Answers may vary.

After the Civil War

1. *The Woman in Battle*
2. She wanted to travel to places she had read about as a child.
3. Nevada, Colorado, New Mexico, and Texas
4. proud of fulfilling her childhood dream

Map Activity: The Battle of Bull Run

1. Pennsylvania, Maryland, and Virginia
2. Circle Bull Run and Washington.
3. approximately 30 miles (1 inch = 25 miles)
4. Add colors to the maps as instructed, and appropriate symbols to the key.

Federico Cavada

Vocabulary Review

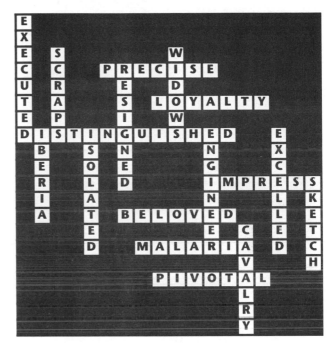

Understanding the Biography

Before the Civil War

1. 1821
2. Cienfuegos, Cuba
3. He moved because his father died and his mother decided to move to Philadelphia to live with her brother.
4. Yes. He was able to communicate with his company in English and the people of Panama in Spanish.

During the Civil War

1. Chantilly, South Mountain, Harper's Ferry, Antietam, Fredericksburg, Chancellorsville, and Gettysburg; also accept Grant's Wilderness Campaign, which was actually a series of battles.
2. He floated in a balloon and used his engineering skills to map and draw pictures of the battles below.

3. the Union's useless charge on Marye's Heights, which resulted in thousands of deaths
4. Answers may vary.

After the Civil War

1. Cuba
2. He trained local Cubans to fight using guerrilla warfare techniques. He wrote a training manual. He became commander-in-chief and captured several Spanish forts.
3. He was captured because he would not leave his wounded friend.
4. Answers may vary.

Map Activity: Escape from Libby Prison

1. through the fireplace
2. a shed across the street
3. 53 feet long
4. 2 feet by 2 feet; 16 inches by 16 inches
5. They probably dug with the shovel and used the box with a rope to pull the dirt out of the tunnel.

Santos Benavides

Vocabulary Review

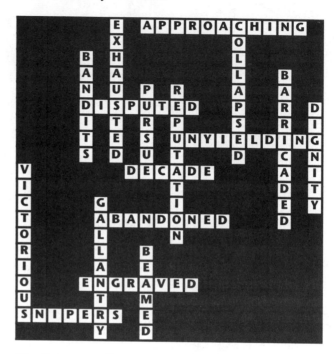

Understanding the Biography

Before the Civil War

1. 1836
2. 1845
3. When Texas was annexed by the United States, the U.S. and Mexico could not agree on where the border should be—the Rio Nueces or the Rio Grande. When Mexico attacked U.S. troops in the disputed territory, a war started between the U.S. and Mexico.
4. Answers may vary.

During the Civil War

1. an engraved pistol
2. He was exhausted from three years of traveling around without adequate food or shelter.
3. He barricaded the streets of Laredo. He put snipers on the rooftops. Then, he and 42 men positioned themselves outside of town.
4. Answers may vary

After the Civil War

1. He turned his attention to business by protecting wagon trains.
2. legislator
3. protecting Laredo from attacks by Indians and bandits; defending Laredo from attacks during the Civil War; serving as a legislator
4. Answers may vary.

Map Activity: The Civil War in Southeastern Texas

1. Color the map as instructed.
2. Battle of Mier, Battle of Camargo
3. about 50 miles
4. Draw lines as instructed; about 300 miles (12 inches, 1 inch = about 25 miles)

Rafael Chacón

Vocabulary Review

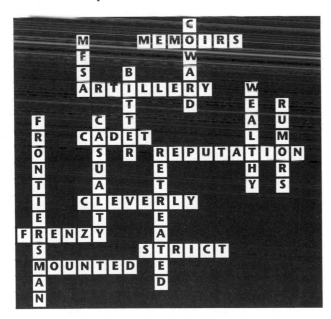

Understanding the Biography

Before the Civil War

1. He learned that honor was the most important thing a person could have.

2. He hid the money in a belt under his shirt.
3. The New Mexican commander ordered his troops, including Chacón, to retreat back to Santa Fe.
4. He continued to travel without complaint, despite the bitter cold and inadequate clothing and shelter. Also, he purposely mounted an officer's horse so he could ride to the front of the battle.

During the Civil War

1. Kit Carson
2. He had a bilingual friend write letters convincing the commanders that they should not take his men's horses away.
3. First, he attacked and successfully captured a Texas artillery piece. Later, he charged and drove the enemy back. When retreating, his company was the last to cross the river to safety.
4. Answers may vary.

After the Civil War

1. He became wealthy raising sheep and cattle on the grassy lands near Trinidad, Colorado.
2. religion, education, and honor
3. Answers may vary.
4. He meant that he did not receive any money from his ancestors, but he received a belief in the importance of honor instead.

Map Activity: The Battle of Valverde

1. Federales – Union or Federals
   Confederados – Confederates
   caballeria – cavalry
   infanteria – infantry
   artilleria – artillery
2. "Plan of the Battle of Valverde. First part. From sunrise until 2:00 in the afternoon, under direct command of Colonel Roberts."
3. *N—Norte* (North,) *O—Oeste* (West), *S—Sur* (South), *E—Este* (East)
4. Label and color as instructed.

5–8. Label and draw as instructed.

Manuel Chaves

Vocabulary Review

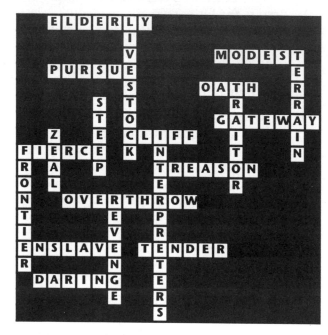

Understanding the Biography

Before the Civil War

1. They were soldiers who explored Central and South America.
2. He learned English while traveling around buying fruit for his business.
3. He showed his courage by walking 200 miles home while wounded from an Indian attack. He showed his fairness by leaving his sickbed to talk his brother out of getting revenge for the attack.
4. Answers may vary.

During the Civil War

1. His first job was protecting Fort Fauntleroy.
2. He learned that Sibley was going to head toward Fort Union through Glorieta Pass.
3. They wanted to conquer New Mexico because it was the gateway to the gold fields of Colorado and California.
4. Answers may vary.

After the Civil War

1. He wanted to return to his peaceful life as a sheep rancher.
2. a journalist named Charles Lummis
3. He was known as *El Lioncito* because he was as brave as a lion.
4. Answers may vary.

Map Activity: New Mexico in the Civil War

1. Arizona, Utah, Texas, and Colorado; Chihuahua
2. Rio Grande
   They traveled along the Rio Grande so they would have access to water for themselves and their horses.
3. between 175 and 200 miles, depending on if the student measures in a straight line or through Albuquerque and Santa Fe
4. The Sangre de Cristo Mountains were in the way.

Multicultural Education for All Students

Public schools in the United States have become increasingly diverse in recent years. Students of color—Native Americans, African Americans, Asian Americans, and Latinos—are now the majority in 23 of the 25 largest school districts in the country. This diversity has led to a movement to modify curriculum and teaching methods, which may not have been adequately addressing the needs of these students. This movement advocates a new approach to teaching called multicultural education.

At the same time, there has been a shift in approaches to the study of history. There has been a dramatic change away from an exclusive focus on the powerful to a focus on all groups that have contributed to historical events. This new perspective, known as social history, has transformed the social science disciplines. In the study of U.S. history in particular, there has been a growing consensus that the achievements of many groups have long been neglected. This has resulted in a demand for changes in the way history is taught in our schools.

Because of this trend, the social studies curriculum has become the cutting edge of multicultural education reform in our schools. Thus, social studies teachers in particular need to ask themselves: What is the most appropriate way to include the lives and experiences of those who have long been excluded?

Banks's Model: Integrating Multicultural Education into the Curriculum

Multicultural education professor James Banks has developed a model of multicultural education that addresses this question. As school districts have grappled with the issue of multicultural curricular reform, they invariably consider a variety of approaches. Banks's model identifies four different levels of multicultural education:

1. **Contributions Approach, or Heroes and Holidays**

This is by far the easiest and most common approach adopted by our schools. Teachers simply add a one-day holiday, like Cinco de Mayo or Martin Luther King Day, to their class without modifying the ongoing curriculum. Even in social studies, the hero or holiday is taught in such a way that it is unrelated to the social studies curriculum. Twentieth-century Latinos or African American achievers might be studied, but they are seen as separate or distinct, and therefore not important to the study of history.

2. **Ethnic Additive Approach**

In this approach, information about an ethnic group related to the curriculum is provided, but it is merely added on at the end—almost as an afterthought. For example, a Native American tribe is added to a unit on westward expansion. But, the curriculum moves on without really considering the equal importance of the perspectives of both the Native Americans and white settlers. A more objective study of this period might focus on the interaction between two different, but equally valid and important cultures clashing on the Great Plains.

3. **Transformation Approach**

This approach marks a fundamental shift from the first two. This approach advocates not just supplementing the current curriculum with heroes, holidays, or groups, but also *integrating* them directly into the curriculum. This integration, or infusion, requires a major change in the organization of the curriculum. Instead of emphasizing how different groups have impacted mainstream U.S. culture and history, the focus is on how many diverse groups have impacted each other on the way to producing the multicultural mosaic of U.S. culture and history.

4. **Decision Making and Social Action**

This is an extension of the transformation approach. After learning about the roles of different groups in U.S. history, the students act on a contemporary problem or issue in their own community.

Banks recognizes that often schools and teachers must move progressively through these stages, and that taking the first approach is better than an exclusively monocultural approach. But, his main point is that the more we integrate or infuse multicultural education directly into our curriculum, the more effective it will be.

Integrating Multicultural Education into the Civil War

The integration of multicultural education into a set curriculum requires a lot of work for teachers. Most textbooks have moved very far in the direction of multiculturalism, but still tend to be organized around an ethnocentric perspective, with other groups added on instead of integrated. Until textbooks fully integrate the achievements of women and minorities, it is left to the teacher to gather the resources needed to fill in any gaps.

If relying exclusively on the textbook to study the Civil War, a true multicultural study of the Civil War following the advanced approaches in Banks's model would not be possible. Although a recent survey of high school U.S. history textbooks found that all mentioned that 180,000 African Americans fought in the war, they varied greatly in the depth of their coverage of this topic. It is up to the teacher to determine whether the textbook needs to be supplemented to implement a transformational approach to the Civil War. For example, books about this topic or movies like Glory could be used to infuse the role of African Americans into a multicultural Civil War study.

Rarely in the current textbooks, however, is there any mention of the role of the 10,000 Latinos who fought. A truly objective, multicultural approach to the Civil War would integrate the achievements of Latinos and other long-neglected groups when talking about the role of Northern and Southern whites in the causes, battles, and aftermath of the war. Students should then gain an appreciation that these groups fought valiantly and courageously—despite the obstacles of prejudice and discrimination, which have kept their achievements hidden for so long.

The role of Latinos has been particularly overlooked for other reasons. Many Latinos lacked the English skills required to add their experience to the history books. In New Mexico, for example, battle reports written in Spanish by Latino officers were routinely ignored by English-speaking commanders. Some of these English-speaking commanders even evaded blame for key defeats by scapegoating the Latino soldiers. Consequently, many primary sources of the period tend to be skewed towards an anti-Latino perspective. Only in recent years have Civil War historians begun to dig deeper to uncover the positive accomplishments of Latino heroes.

Conversely, many well-intentioned textbooks fail to point out the Hispanic heritage of fluent English-speaking, assimilated Latino heroes like Admiral David Farragut. His accomplishments are well documented, but his heritage is ignored.

I hope this book will be a helpful resource for those teachers aiming to infuse a Civil War study with the accomplishments of all groups.

Strategies for Using This Book with English Learners

This book has been written in such a way as to make it accessible to a wide range of students. However, it is especially adaptable to the needs of students who are learning a second language. These limited English proficient (LEP) students, or English learners, share many similar needs, which are addressed in this book. The following information is intended to provide a foundation on which a teacher can effectively meet these unique needs.

English Learners and the Stages of Language Acquisition

Educational researchers Krashen and Terrell developed a model of second-language acquisition that mirrors the way a child acquires a first language. Anyone who has observed a child growing up knows that language develops according to universal stages: a silent period, one-word utterances, short phrases, and finally whole sentences. Krashen and Terrell propose that a person of any age acquires a second language in a similar way. They have defined the following stages:

I. Preproduction or Comprehension Stage

Language learners begin to acquire a second language by listening to language. In a classroom, these students can respond with physical actions, but are not ready to answer questions orally.

II. Early Production Stage

At this stage, language learners begin to produce basic words. They can respond to teachers' questions with one-word answers (such as yes/no) or prompted choices by the teacher (for example, Is he young or old?).

III. Speech Emergence Stage

At this point, language students will produce increasingly longer and more complex phrases. They may be able to respond to questions with whole sentences and participate in basic reading and writing activities.

IV. Intermediate Fluency Stage

Language learners can now speak with relative ease, though there are still noticeable gaps in vocabulary and syntax. Reading and writing activities can become much more extensive at this point.

V. Advanced Fluency Stage

Students at this stage basically reach a level in which they are roughly equivalent to the mainstream English speaker. Reading and writing skills, however, will still not be as advanced as speaking skills.

What, then, is required for English learners to successfully move from one stage to the next? According to Krashen, the key element is that the students receive sufficient amounts of what is known as *comprehensible input*.

Comprehensible Input: Sheltered Social Studies Techniques

Comprehensible input refers to the provision of language that is within the English learner's realm of understanding. Language input too far above the current stage of development is unlikely to be comprehended, and it is, therefore, not helpful to language acquisition. If, for example, English learners at Stage I or II listen to an English talk show for hours, they are unlikely to learn any English from it, because the input will not be comprehensible. It will just be "noise." If, on the other hand, the same students listen to a teacher presenting the same topic, using a modified delivery approach known as sheltered instruction, they will receive the comprehensible input required to progress to the next stage of language acquisition.

Sheltered instruction techniques include the following:

- modified vocabulary and syntax
- repetition of key points and new vocabulary
- slower pacing
- use of body language to describe content
- use of visuals such as pictures, maps, charts, and video clips

In short, sheltered instruction is the provision of comprehensible input in academic content classes like social studies, science, and math.

The text and follow-up activities in this book are specifically designed so that they can be presented in a sheltered as well as a mainstream social studies class. English learners at language acquisition Stage III and above would benefit the most. English learners at Stages I and II would be better served by similar material in their native language, so that they do not fall behind in academic content while acquiring basic English skills. However, if paired off with more fluent bilingual students, they could participate.

Latino Heroes of the Civil War contains several features that enable it to be used as a vehicle for comprehensible input. The following is a list of how different features can be effectively utilized for English learners:

Glossary

Each biography has been written with a conscious attempt to control the vocabulary without watering down the content. In addition, each biography includes a glossary of 15 to 20 words, which may be difficult for English learners in Stages III and above. Of course, students at lower stages will not be familiar with many of the words.

Vocabulary Review Puzzle

The same words defined in the glossary are reinforced in this activity. Each word is placed in a sentence, which forces the English learner to apply the new word to a real-life modern context.

Understanding the Biography

The comprehension questions in this section are organized to be progressively more difficult. They not only follow Bloom's taxonomy but also parallel the stages of language acquisition. Thus,

English learners at lower stages should only have to answer the first or second questions in each part (Before, During, and After), while the more advanced students can be expected to answer all of the questions.

Map Activity

These activities are excellent tools for sheltered instruction. The maps help the English learner visualize an aspect of the biography while applying a number of different map skills. Like the comprehension questions, they are usually organized so that they are progressively more difficult. English learners at lower stages could respond to the teacher's instructions by labeling, coloring, or illustrating—as described in the map questions.

Time Line and Map Templates

These resources enable students to demonstrate an understanding of the sheltered comprehensible input of the teacher. As the teacher or students read through a biography, the students can use these templates to record information about key events in the biography.

All of these features, plus the pictures included in each biography, will help to facilitate comprehensible input. However, in order to see that successful language acquisition is occurring, the comprehensible input must lead to *comprehensible output*.

Comprehensible Output

The goal of providing comprehensible input is eventually to have the students produce the language themselves. There are two techniques which can facilitate this process: scaffolding and cooperative learning. While these techniques can be very effective with fluent English proficient students, they are especially useful to English learners.

Scaffolding

Scaffolding refers to the idea that students will successfully develop skills if we provide a lot of initial support and then gradually withdraw support until the student can be successful independently. A typical lesson or unit would proceed from teacher modeling to group or partner activities, and then to an independent activity. In applying this to English language development, the teacher should begin by modeling while using the sheltered techniques necessary to make the input comprehensible. Then, some kind of interactive guided group practice should be used so that the English learner can continue to receive comprehensible input from teachers and peers while starting to produce their own language (comprehensible output). Finally, individual students are expected to produce something on their own that extends directly from the comprehensible input and the teacher and group.

For example, in using one of the biographies in this book, the teacher would begin by reading the first section, Before the Civil War. He or she would then model how to answer the corresponding questions in Understanding the Biography and competing the appropriate parts of the Time Line and Map templates. The next scaffolding step is guided group practice. Students then get into groups to complete the same activities after reading the second section of the biography, During the Civil War. Students in the groups may help each other and get help from the teacher at this point. The last scaffolding step is individualized production. Students complete on their own the same activities corresponding to the last section of the biography, After the Civil War. Thus, at the end of this scaffolding sequence, students will be producing comprehensible output.

Cooperative Learning

Cooperative learning is another effective technique for facilitating comprehensible output. It is a specific type of group work that can be incorporated into the second step of scaffolding. Many books are available on the basics of this teaching strategy, but I would like to emphasize the importance of one aspect for English learners: **positive interdependence**.

This refers to the idea that each student in a cooperative group is responsible for a part of a whole group project. Usually, each group member either has a specific job or is responsible for completing one specific section of a larger project. Either way, the group members are interdependent—they must work together to produce a final product. Each is responsible for a part or job, but can get help from other group members. Thus, this is an excellent strategy to use with the guided group practice step of scaffolding.

In sum, comprehensible output is facilitated when a learning project proceeds through these scaffolding steps:

1. **Modeling with Sheltered Instruction**

Actively demonstrate to the students what you want them to do. Walk through the project step-by-step, showing the students how to do something by using sheltered techniques—body language, visuals, repetition, controlled vocabulary, and so forth.

2. **Guided Group Practice with Positive Interdependence**

Assign students tasks that follow the same sequence as the one modeled. The skill necessary to complete the task should be the same, but the content or topic differs. Students are in cooperative groups with positive interdependence, and the teacher can assist as needed. This step is the bridge to the next step.

3. **Individual Products As the Goal**

After each student has contributed to a part of a whole project in step 2, they are ready to attempt to produce it on their own. Again, the skills necessary to complete the tasks should be similar to those completed in steps 1 and 2, but the content differs.

The following section provides the details of an assessment project that utilizes all of the concepts described thus far.

Assessment Project: Latino Heroes Action Comic Book

In order to adequately assess a student's progress, a variety of assessment tools are needed. Reliance on tests alone does not necessarily give a teacher a complete picture of a student's knowledge and skills. Recently, educators have moved toward incorporating what is called **authentic assessment** into the grading process. Authentic assessment emphasizes the judging of a student's progress through the application of knowledge and skills to a creative project. Each of the biographies in this book has a creative project to assist in assessment. However, teachers may find that they can attain greater success with their students through a long-term assessment project utilizing scaffolding.

The technique of scaffolding was described in depth in the previous section on Strategies for English Learners. However, like so many of these strategies, it is also an excellent teaching strategy for mainstream students. To review, the basic principle of scaffolding is that all good teaching of skills should proceed through three stages:

1. teacher modeling
2. guided group practice
3. individual production

In following these three steps, the teacher is gradually withdrawing support (or the scaffold), with the goal of promoting individual student success with certain targeted skills. Thus, the teacher can assess individual attainment of skills developed over a period of time. The skills remain constant through the three scaffolding steps, only the content varies.

Project Objectives

- Students will create an action comic book summarizing a Latino hero's life.
- Students will complete a parallel time line.
- Students will use an atlas to locate and label events on a map.

Scaffolding Step One: Teacher-Modeled Class Project

Materials Needed (see Teacher Resources for Assessment Project)

- Farragut biography for each student
- U.S. and World Map template for each student
- 19th-Century Time Line template transparency
- U.S. and World Map template transparencies
- Storyboard template transparency
- Overhead projector
- Colored overhead markers
- Nine sheets of 8½" × 11" drawing paper
- Atlas (class set optional)

Purpose

In this step, the teacher models the skills. By the end of this step, students are working cooperatively in a groups to produce one page of a comic book.

Procedures

1. Read the text of the Farragut biography with the whole class. Model strategies for using context clues and the Glossary to learn new vocabulary.
2. Put the Nineteenth-Century Time Line template on the overhead. Discuss the nineteenth-century events listed on the left side. Ask students to find specific dates of important events in Farragut's life. Show students how to mark events on the right side of the time line.
3. Put the U.S. and World Map templates on the overhead. Model, using the atlas to locate the events from the time line. Select one color, and use it to label the key places

mentioned in the biography. Use the same color to indicate the likely routes Farragut took on his travels. Add a key with the color and Farragut's name. Tell students to work individually on their own map while you model. This same map will be used later to label other heroes' travels.

4. Put the Storyboard template on the overhead. Select nine events from the time line, and write one date and event in each storyboard panel.

5. Take the first event and write it on the bottom of a sheet of drawing paper. Draw a more detailed, colorful picture of the event. Be sure to color the whole paper to give it the look of a comic book page. Add speech bubbles with dialogue from the characters in the pictures.

6. Divide the class into eight groups with approximately four students in each group. Give each group one piece of drawing paper. Assign each group one of the eight remaining events in the storyboard.

7. Model while each group completes the storyboard. If using cooperative learning at this stage, you may want to assign these jobs:
   - writer—writes on group's paper
   - checker—checks to make sure the words are correct
   - artist—draws pictures
   - coordinator—monitors progress and helps as needed

   Have students color the panel and. Of course, you should help as needed.

8. Have each group act out their event in Farragut's life, with a narrator reading the event and actors performing and delivering the brief dialogue in the speech bubbles.

9. Put the nine pages together for a class Action Comic Book of David Farragut's heroic life. Laminate it, and add it to your class library for other students to read and enjoy.

Scaffolding Step Two: Guided Group Project

> **Materials Needed**
> **(see Teacher Resources for Assessment Project)**

- Six copies of five other *Latino Heroes of the Civil War* biographies
- Nineteenth-Century Time Line template for each group
- Storyboard template for each group
- U.S. and World Map templates from Scaffolding Step One
- Nine sheets of $8\frac{1}{2}$" × 11" drawing paper for each group
- Colored pencils, markers, or crayons for each group
- Atlas for each group

> **Purpose**

In this section, the students apply the skills modeled by the teacher in cooperative groups with positive interdependence. By the end of this step, students are working individually to produce one to two pages of a comic book.

> **Procedures**

1. Make five groups with about six students in each group.

2. Assign each group one of the five other Latino heroes of the Civil War.

3. Pair students up and assign partners a section of the biography to read. This can be easily done by assigning each set of partners the sections Before the Civil War, During the Civil War, and After the Civil War. Since During the Civil War is the longest section, you may want to assign this to the strongest readers in the group.

4. Have group members or partners read their section of the biography. Tell partners either to divide up their section or to work together.

5. Ask group members to fill in major events from their section on the time line.

6. Encourage students to use an atlas to locate the places mentioned in the group's time line. Have students use the same map templates from Step One, but a different color to mark locations of important events. Tell them to add the color and the Latino hero's name to the map key.

7. Instruct the group to decide together which are the nine most important events from the Latino hero's life. See that each student is responsible for creating one to two large panels, complete with the date, description, illustration and speech bubbles.

8. Have groups practice and then act out the entire biography.

Scaffolding Step Three: Individual Project

> **Materials Needed**
> **(see Teacher Resources for Assessment Project)**

- Books, reference materials related to twentieth-century Latino heroes
- Twentieth-Century Time Line template for each student
- Storyboard template for each student
- U.S. and World Map Templates from Step One
- Nine sheets of $8\frac{1}{2}$" × 11" drawing paper for each student
- Colored pencils, markers, or crayons for each student
- Atlas for each student

Note on Materials: Because of the prevalence of information available, the individual phase of this assessment project focuses on Latino heroes of the twentieth century. Gather information from a variety of sources. There are many biographies, texts, reference books, and web sites with information on twentieth-century Latino heroes. This book lists some of the more famous people along with a bibliography to assist you in compiling the sources. The list is limited to Latino heroes living in the United States, since that is the focus of this book. Many of the books are available in libraries or through major catalogues.

> **Purpose**

In this section, the students apply the skills learned in groups to an individual project. By the end of this step, students are working individually to produce an entire comic book independently. The product is then used to assess the student's acquisition of skills.

> **Procedures**

1. Compile a list of enough Latino heroes for each student in your class. If you have multiple classes and not enough Latino heroes, you can either duplicate assignments or extend the project to include heroes from other ethnicities.

2. Have individual students choose a hero from the list.

3. Instruct students to read about the hero's life before becoming famous, the hero's major accomplishments, and the events later in the hero's life.

4. Ask each student to complete a new time line using the Twentieth-Century Time Line template.

5. Have each student add the new hero to the Map templates. You may want to have them modify the U.S. Map to reflect the twentieth-century states.

6. Have each student complete the storyboard for the hero, with dialogue, events, and pictures.

7. Request each student to complete the nine-page comic book. This is the final project to be turned in (along with the time line and maps) for assessment.

> **Assessment**

Scaffolding has enabled individual students to eventually accomplish something independently which may not have been possible at the beginning. Evaluate the final project for accuracy, completeness, and creativity. The skills can then be applied to other topics throughout the year.

Teacher Resources for Assessment Project

The following reproducible pages contain various resources for use in the assessment project. However, many can also be used with the biographies in this and other books.

- Time Line of Nineteenth-Century U.S. History
- Time Line of Twentieth-Century U.S. History
- U.S. Map template
- World Map template
- Comic Book Activity Storyboard
- Twentieth-Century U.S. Latino Heroes: Past and Present
- Books on U.S. Latino Heroes of the Twentieth Century

Time Line of Nineteenth-Century
U.S. History

Mark the most important dates in the Latino hero's life on the right side of this time line of nineteenth-century history.

Major Events in U.S. History   **Latino Hero:** _____

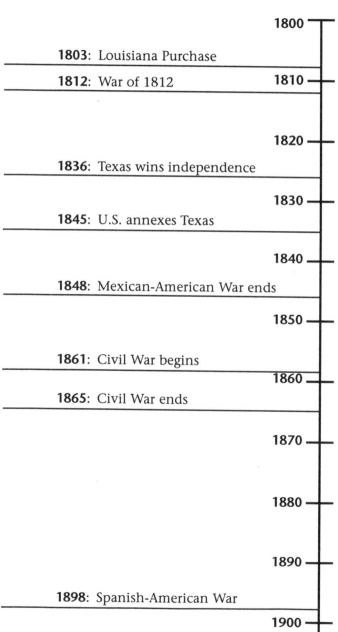

1800

1803: Louisiana Purchase

1812: War of 1812   1810

1820

1836: Texas wins independence

1830

1845: U.S. annexes Texas

1840

1848: Mexican-American War ends

1850

1861: Civil War begins

1860

1865: Civil War ends

1870

1880

1890

1898: Spanish-American War

1900

Time Line of Twentieth-Century
U.S. History

Mark the most important dates in the Latino hero's life on the right side of this time line of twentieth-century history.

Major Events in U.S. History   **Latino Hero:** _____

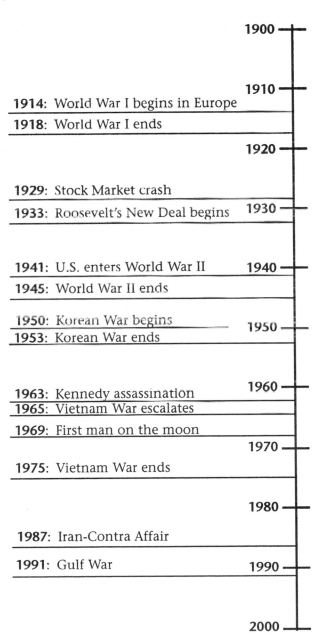

1900

1910

1914: World War I begins in Europe

1918: World War I ends

1920

1929: Stock Market crash

1933: Roosevelt's New Deal begins   **1930**

1941: U.S. enters World War II   **1940**

1945: World War II ends

1950: Korean War begins

1953: Korean War ends   **1950**

1963: Kennedy assassination   **1960**

1965: Vietnam War escalates

1969: First man on the moon

1970

1975: Vietnam War ends

1980

1987: Iran-Contra Affair

1991: Gulf War   **1990**

2000

Name _____ Date _____

U.S. Map Template

Label all the places in the United States that the Latino hero visited in his or her life. Use lines with arrows to show the routes he or she traveled. If labeling more than one hero, use a different color for each one. Make a key showing whom each color represents.

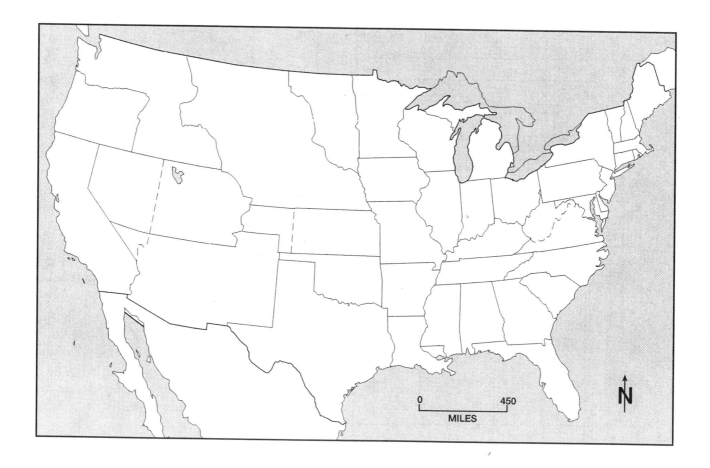

       Latino Heroes of the Civil War

Name _____   Date _____

World Map Template

Label all the places in the world that the Latino hero visited in his or her life. Use lines with arrows to show the routes he or she traveled. If labeling more than one hero, use a different color for each one. Make a key showing whom each color represents.

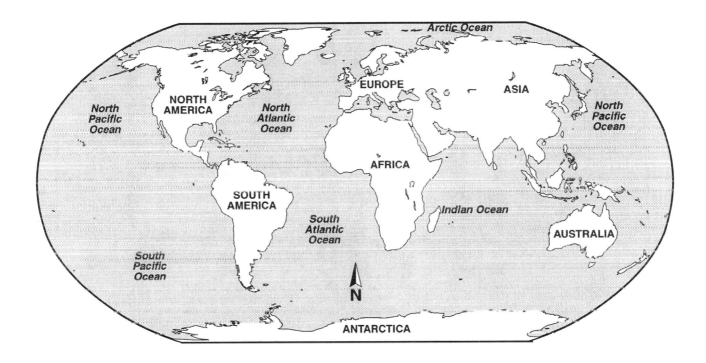

Name _____ Date _____

Comic Book Storyboard

Use this storyboard to depict nine events from the life of a Latino hero. Each box should include a date, a one-sentence description of the event, and a drawing with speech bubbles showing what the characters say.

Twentieth-Century U.S. Latino Heroes: Past and Present

The following is a partial list of Latino heroes and heroines who have made significant contributions in their respective fields during the 1900's. They all lived in the United States during the time of their success. Though each excelled in a particular field of endeavor, they may not have necessarily risked their lives, as did the Civil War heroes featured in this book. However, by overcoming obstacles and rising to the top of their fields, they each demonstrated the qualities that mark someone as a hero.

Twentieth-Century Latino Heroes of the Past

Hero	Field	Born–Died
Arnaz, Desi	TV, Film, Music	1917–1986
Alvarez, Luis	Physics	1911–1988
Bori, Lucrezia	Opera	1888–1960
Casals, Pablo	Classical Music	1876–1973
Castaneda, Carlos	History	1896–1958
Cháves, César	Labor, Civil Rights	1927–1993
Cháves, Dennis	Politics	1888–1962
Clemente, Roberto	Baseball	1934–1972
Cubría, Mercedes	Military	1903–1980
Cugat, Xavier	Music	1900–1990
Fernández, Antonio Manuel	Politics	1902–1956
Gutierrez, Juan	Medical Researcher	1852–1925
Hayworth, Rita (b. Rita Cansino)	Film	1918–1987
Lamas, Fernando	Film	1915–1982
Lázaro, Ladislas	Politics	1872–1927
Marín, Luis Muñoz	Politics	1898–1980
Ochoa, Severo	Physicist	1895–1993
Santayana, George	Philosophy, Writing	1863–1952
Valens, Ritchie (b. Valenzuela)	Popular Music	1942–1959

(continued)

Twentieth-Century U.S. Latino Heroes: Past and Present

Twentieth-Century Latino Heroes of the Present

Hero	Field	Born
Aguirre, Michael	Law	1949
Alvarado, Linda	Business	1951
Alvarez, Everett	Military	1937
Alvarez, Julia	Literature	1951
Anaya, Rudolfo	Writer	1937
Arciniega, Tomás	Higher Education	1937
Arreola, Philip	Law Enforcement	1940
Baca, Judith	Art	1946
Baez, Joan	Popular Music	1941
Barro, Mary Helen	Radio Broadcasting	1938
Benavides, Roy	Military	1935
Blades, Rubén	Popular Music and Film	1948
Bonilla, Tony	Civil Rights	1936
Bujones, Fernando	Ballet Dancing	1955
Bustamante, Cruz	Politics	1933
Cabranés, José	Justice	1940
Caicedo, Harry	Journalism	1928
Carr, Vikki	Popular Music	1940
Carter, Linda Córdoba	Television, Film	1951?
Cavazos, Lauro	Higher Education	1927
Chang-Diaz, Franklin	Astronaut	1950
Cisneros, Evelyn	Ballet Dancing	1958
Cisneros, Henry	Politics	1947
Cisneros, Sandra	Literature	1954
Corona, Bert	Labor Organizer	1918
Coronado, José	Health Care	1932
Corral, Edward	Fire Fighting	1931
Cruz, Celia	Latin Music	1929
Escalante, Jaime	Education	1930
Estefan, Gloria	Music	1958
Estés, Clarissa Pinkola	Psychiatry, Writing	1943
Fernández, Joseph	Education	1936
Fernández, Ricardo	Higher Education	1940
Flores, Patrick	Religion	1929

(continued)

Twentieth-Century U.S. Latino Heroes: Past and Present

Hero	Field	Born
Galarza, Ernesto	Education, Labor	1905
García, Hector Pérez	Civil Rights	1914
Garza, Kika de la	Politics	1927
Garza, Reynaldo	Judiciary	1915
Goizueta, Roberto	Business	1931
Gómez, Elsa	Higher Education	1938
González, Henry	Politics	1916
Gonzalez, Pancho	Tennis	1928
González, Raymond E.	Diplomacy	1924
Guzmán, Suzanna	Classical Music	1955
Guerrero, Lena	Government	1957
Hernández, Antonia	Law, Civil Rights	1948
Hernández, Diego Edyl	Military	1934
Herrera, Carolina	Fashion	1939
Hijuelos, Oscar	Literature	1951
Huerta, Dolores	Union Organizer, Lobbyist	1930
Juliá, Raúl	Theater, Film	1940
León, Tania	Classical Music	1943
Lopez, Nancy	Golf	1957
Luján, Manuel	Politics, Government	1928
Maidique, Modesto	Higher Education, Business	1940
Marisol	Art	1930
Martinez, Vilma	Law, Civil Rights	1943
Mata, Eduardo	Classical Music	1942
Mohr, Nicholasa	Literature	1938
Montalbán, Ricardo	Film	1920
Moreno, Rita	Theater, Film	1931
Nava, Julián	Educator, Ambassador	1927
Nevárez, Miguel	Higher Education	1937
Novello, Antonia Coello	Health Care	1944
Obledo, Mario	Law, Politics	1932
Ocampo, Adriana	Planetary Geology	1955
Ochoa, Ellen	Astronaut	1958
Olmos, Edward James	Theater, Film	1947

(continued)

Twentieth-Century U.S. Latino Heroes: Past and Present

Hero	Field	Born
Orozco, Raymond	Fire Fighting	1933
Ortega, Katherine	Banking	1934
Ortiz, Francis	Diplomacy	1926
Pacheco, Manuel Trinidad	Higher Education	1941
Peña, Federico	Politics, Government	1947
Pérez, Minerva	Television Journalism	1955
Plunkett, Jim	Football	1947
Puentes, Tito	Latin Music	1923
Quinn, Anthony	Film	1915
Quintanilla, Guadalupe	Higher Education	1937
Ramírez, Mario	Medicine	1926
Renta, Oscar de la	Fashion	1932
Reynoso, Cruz	Judiciary	1931
Richardson, Bill	Politics, Diplomacy	1947
Rivera, Geraldo	Journalism, Television	1943
Rodríguez, Gloria	Education	1948
Rodríguez, Paul	Entertainment	19--*
Rodriguez, Richard	Journalism, Writing	1948
Romero, César	Film	1907
Ronstadt, Linda	Music	1946
Roybal, Edward	Politics	1916
Santana, Carlos	Rock Music	1947
Sateiro, Luis	TV Writer, Playwright	1947
Saralegui, Cristina	Television, Journalism	1948
Serrano, Alberto	Psychiatry	1931
Sheen, Martin	Film	1940
Suárez, Javier	Politics	1949
Suárez, Robert	Journalism	1928
Torres, Art	Politics	1941
Valdez, Luis	Theater	1940
Velázquez, Nydia	Education, Government	1953
Villalpando, Catalina	Treasurer	1940
Welch, Raquel (b. Tejada)	Film	1940

*Date unavailable

Latino Heroes of the Civil War

Books on U.S. Latino Heroes of the Twentieth Century

The following books contain biographical information on prominent Latinos in the United States. Since they all emphasize heroic Latinos of the twentieth-century, they can be used as resources for the individual stage of the assessment project, or for general reference.

Biographical Collections

Allen, Angela. *Focus on Hispanic Americans.* Westminster: Teacher Created Materials, 1995.

Cockcroft, James. *Latinos in the Making of the United States (The Hispanic Experience in the Americas).* Danbury, CT: Franklin Watts, 1995.

Levadi, Barbara (ed.). *Latino Biographies.* Paramus, NJ: Globe Fearon, 1995.

Lobb, Nancy. *16 Extraordinary Hispanic Americans.* Portland, ME: J. Weston Walch, 1995.

Machamer, Gene. *Hispanic American Profiles.* Westminster, MD: Random House, Inc., 1996.

Marquez, Nancy. *Portraits of Mexican-Americans.* Parsippany, NJ: Good Apple, 1991.

Meier, Matt, et al. *Notable Latino Americans: A Biographical Dictionary.* Westport, CT: Greenwood, 1997.

Morey, Janet and Dunn, Wendy. *Famous Hispanic Americans.* New York: Cobblehill, 1996.

Palacios, Argentina. *Standing Tall: The Stories of Ten Hispanic Americans.* New York: Scholastic, 1994.

Sinnot, Susan. *Extraordinary Hispanic Americans.* Chicago: Childrens Press, 1995.

Telgen, Diane. *Latinas! Women of Achievement.* Anchorage, AK: Visible Ink Press, 1996.

Reference Books with Biographical Information

Chabrán, Richard and Chabrán, Rafael, ed. *The Latino Encyclopedia*, 6 volumes. Tarrytown, NY: Marshall Cavendish Corp., 1996.

Kanellos, Nicolás. *The Hispanic Almanac: From Columbus to Corporate America.* Anchorage, AK: Visible Ink Press, 1994.

Kanellos, Nicolás and Perez, Cristelia. *Chronology of Hispanic-American History: From Pre-Columbian Times to the Present.* Detroit: Gale Research, 1995.

Novas, Himilce. *The Hispanic 100: A Ranking of the Latino Men and Women Who Have Most Influenced American Thought and Culture.* Secaucus, NJ: Citadel Press, 1995.

Tardiff, Joseph, and Mabunda, L. Mpho, eds. *Dictionary of Hispanic Biography.* Detroit: Gale Research, 1996.

Unterberger, Amy, ed. *Who's Who Among Hispanic Americans, 1994–1995*, 3rd Edition. Detroit: Gale Research, 1994.

Textbooks with Biographical Information

Hispanics in U.S. History, Vol 2: 1865 to Present. Englewood Cliffs, NJ. Globe Book Company, 1989.

The Latino Experience in U.S. History. Paramus, NJ: Globe Fearon, 1994.

Biographical Book Series

Hispanics of Achievement. (20 biographies). New York: Chelsea House, 1991–1992.

Marvis, Barbara. *Famous People of Hispanic Heritage* (six volumes). Elktown, MD: Mitchell Lane Publications, 1995.

Hispanic Stories. (15 biographies). Austin, TX: Raintree/Steck-Vaughn, 1991–1993.

Appendixes

Appendix A—Web Sites on Latino Heroes

In the mid-nineties, as the Internet's World Wide Web exploded nationwide, a number of excellent web sites were developed, that could be helpful to anyone researching Latino heroes. Since new web sites go up every day, the following should not be considered a comprehensive list. Rather, it represents the best as of April 1997.

Site name: *Famous Hispanics*

URL address: http://www.clark.net/pub/jgbustam/famosos.html

Description: This site contains a comprehensive list of past and present Latino heroes. It has an alphabetical list of over 200 Latinos, plus separate lists organized by categories: Antiquity, Musicians, Nobel Prizes, Painters, Scientists, Sports, Military, Women, and Writers. There is a short, paragraph-long biographical sketch of each Latino. Many of the Latino heroes are from countries outside the United States.

Site name: *Quien es Quien*

URL address: http://clnet.ucr.edu/research/quien.html

Description: This site contains links to other sites about Latino heroes. The link for César Cháves is excellent and comprehensive—a long biography, chronology, downloadable sound clips (in English and Spanish), pictures, and documents.

Site name: *Hispanic America USA—An Overview of Our Nation's Defense: The Military Heritage of Hispanic Americans*

URL address: http://www.neta.com/~1stbooks/defensl.htm

Description: This site contains brief sketches about dozens of Latino military heroes from the *conquistadores* to Vietnam. It also includes an interesting page about "Hero Street," a small street in Illinois which has sent 84 Latinos to fight in America's wars.

Site name: *Hispanic America USA—Medal of Honor Recipients*

URL address: http://www.neta.com/~1stbooks/medal.htm

Description: This page, part of the previous site, lists Latino military heroes who have received the Congressional Medal of Honor. Most listings have short summaries of each winner's heroic accomplishment. Some have pictures.

Appendix B—Guide to Military Ranks

The following are the most common military ranks that existed at the end of the Civil War, from highest to lowest. Many of these ranks are used throughout the book.

Common Military Ranks			
Army		**Navy**	
Officers	**Enlisted Personnel**	**Officers**	**Enlisted Personnel**
general	sergeant major	admiral	midshipman (seaman training to be an officer)
colonel	sergeant	vice admiral	seaman
lieutenant colonel	corporal	rear admiral	
major	private	commodore	
captain		captain	
lieutenant		lieutenant	

Appendix C—Latinos in the Civil War: Congressional Medal of Honor Recipients

Many Latinos besides the six featured in this book fought heroically in the Civil War. Three Latinos even won the Congressional Medal of Honor. According to the Congressional Medal of Honor Society, this award is "the highest award for valor in action that this nation awards its servicemen." The deed must be an outstanding and verified act of gallantry in which the soldier risked his or her life. The Civil War was the first war in which the medal was given out. At the time, only enlisted men, not officers, could receive it. Therefore, the six Latino Heroes in this book would not have been eligible, since they were officers—or, in the case of Loreta Velázquez, not officially enlisted.

Joseph De Castro

Rank: Corporal

This hero was born in Boston, Massachusetts, on November 14, 1844. He fought in the Union Army of the Potomac at the Battle of Gettysburg in Pennsylvania. He received his medal for capturing the flag of the Confederate's 19th Virginia Regiment on July 3, 1863. He died May 8, 1892.

Philip Bazaar

Rank: Ordinary seaman

This hero was born in Chile and moved to New Bedford, Massachusetts. He was stationed on the U.S.S. *Santiago de Cuba* during an attack on Fort Fisher in North Carolina, near the end of the war. On January 15, 1865, he was one of six men to bravely sail ashore in a small boat and enter the fort. He also risked his life carrying dispatches during the heat of the battle.

John Ortega

Rank: Seaman and Master's Mate

This hero was born in Spain in 1840, but grew up in Pennsylvania. During the Civil War, he served aboard the U.S.S. *Saratoga*. He distinguished himself during two actions and was promoted to master's mate as a result.

Bibliography

American Heritage Junior Library: Naval Battles and Heroes. New York: American Heritage Publishing Co., Inc., 1960.

Banks, James. *Multicultural Education: Theory and Practice,* 3rd Edition. Boston: Allyn and Bacon, 1994.

Cavada, Federico F. *Libby Life—Experiences of a Prisoner of War.* 1865; rpt. Lanham, MD: University Press of America, 1985.

Colton, Ray L. *The Civil War in the Western Territories.* Norman, OK: University of Oklahoma Press, 1959.

De Varona, Frank. *Hispanic Presence in the United States: Historical Beginnings.* Miami: Mnemosyn Publishing Co., 1993.

Farragut, Loyall. *The Life of David Glasgow Farragut, First Admiral of the United States Navy, Embodying his Journal and Letters.* New York: D. Appleton and Company, 1879.

Hispanics in the Civil War. (brochure) Washington, D.C.: Parks and History Association, 1991

Hispanics in U.S. History, Vol. 1: Through 1865. Englewood Cliffs, NJ: Globe Book Company, 1989.

Josephy, Alvin M. *The Civil War in the American West.* New York: Alfred A. Knopf, 1991.

Krashen, Stephen, and Terrell, Tracy. *The Natural Approach: Language Acquisition in the Classroom.* Oxford: Pergamon Press, date.

The Latino Experience in U.S. History. Paramus, NJ: Globe Fearon, 1994.

Lewis, Charles Lee. *David Glasgow Farragut—Admiral in the Making.* Annapolis, MD: U.S. Naval Institute, 1941.

____. *David Glasgow Farragut—Our First Admiral.* Annapolis, MD: U.S. Naval Institute, 1941.

Loewen, James W. *Lies My Teacher Told Me.: Everything Your American History Textbook Got Wrong.* New York: The New Press, 1995.

Martin, Christopher. *Damn the Torpedoes! The Story of America's First Admiral: David Glasgow Farragut.* London: Abelard-Schuman, 1970.

Mekeh, Jacqueline, ed. *Legacy of Honor: The Life of Rafael Chacón, A Nineteenth-Century New Mexican.* Albuquerque: University of New Mexico Press, 1986.

Miller, Darlis A. "Hispanos and the Civil War in New Mexico: A Reconsideration." *New Mexico Historical Review,* Vol. 54:2, 1979.

Riley, John Denny. "Santos Benavides: His Influence on the Lower Rio Grande, 1823–1891." Ph.D. Thesis, Texas Christian University, 1976.

Scott, Robert. *Glory, Glory, Glorieta.* Boulder, CO: Johnson Printing Co., 1992.

Simmons, Marc. *Little Lion of the Southwest: A Life of Manuel Antonio Chaves.* Chicago: Sage Books, the Shallow Press, Inc., 1973.

Sinnot, Susan. *Extraordinary Hispanic Americans.* Chicago: Childrens Press, 1995.

Stanley, Francis. *The Civil War in New Mexico.* Denver: World Press, 1960.

Thompson, Jerry D. *Mexican Texans in the Union Army.* El Paso: Texas Western Press, 1986.

————. *Vaqueros in Blue and Gray.* Austin, TX: Presidial Press, 1976.

————. *Desert Tiger Captain Paddy Graydon and the Civil War in the Far Southwest.* El Paso, TX: Texas Western Press, 1992.

Vandiver, Frank E. "Civil War, U.S." *Grolier International Encyclopedia.* Danbury, CT: Grolier Incorporated, 1993.

Velázquez, Loreta. *The Woman in Battle.* 1876; rpt. New York: Arno Press, 1972.

Index

A

Admiral Osario, 38
Antietam, 8
Appomattox Courthouse, 9

B

Battle of
    Glorieta Pass, 48
    Taos, 75
    Valverde, 63
Battle of Ball's Bluff, 24
Battle of Bull Run, 8
Battle of Fort Donaldson, 24
Battle of Mobile Bay, 13
Battle of New Orleans, 12
Battles of
    Antietam, 36
    Chantilly, 36
    Fredericksburg, 36
    Harper's Ferry, 36
    South Mountain, 36
Benavides, Jose Jesus, 49
Birney, David, 35
Buford, Harry T., 23

C

Carson, Kit, 62
Cavada, Don Isidro Fernandez, 34
Chacón, Don Albino, 61
Chaves, Amador, 78
Chaves, Julián, 73
Chaves, Manuel, 78
Chavez, Cesar, 2
Chivington, John, 76
Civil War Generals
    Burnside, 38
    McLellan, 38
    Meade, 38
Company K, 62

Coronado, Francisco, 2
Cortés, 21
Cortina, Juan, 51
Cuba's Ten Year's War, 34
Cuban Revolutionary Army, 37

D

de Gálvez, Bernardo, 3
de la Garza, Cayetano, 52
de Miralles, Juan, 3
de Soto, Hernando, 2

E

El Lioncito, 73–78
Emancipation Proclamation, 9

F

Farragut, David, 3
Farragut, Jorge, 3
Federalist War in Mexico, 50
Fish, Hamilton, 38
Ford, John "Rip", 51
Fort Sumter, 5

G

García, María Luz, 73
General
    Bee, 52
Gettysburg, 9
Goodwin, John I., 65
Grant, Ulysses S., 8

H

Hernández, Joseph, 3
Houard, Emelie, 34

I

Indian Wars, 62

J

Jackson, Stonewall, 8
Joan of Arc, 22

L

Labadie, María Vicenta, 74
Las Bocas, 37
Lee, Robert E., 8
Libby Concentration Camp, 36
Libby Life, 37

M

Manifest Destiny, 4
Marye's Heights, 36
Meade, George, 36
Mexican War, 61
Missouri Compromise, 4

P

Pickett's Charge, 9

Polk, James, 4
Ponce de León, Juan, 2

R

Román, Don, 78

S

Sanchez, Tomás, 49
Sherman, William, 9
Shiloh, 8
Sibley, Henry, 48

T

Tecumseh, 12
Ten Year's War, 37

V

Villareal, Augustina, 50

W

Wilderness Campaign, 37

About the Author

Mike Walbridge is a bilingual mentor teacher at Frisbie Middle School in Rialto, California. During his 11 years as an educator, he has taught English as a Second Language, Sheltered Social Studies, and mainstream social studies to students from second to tenth grade. He graduated with a major in political science from the University of California at Berkeley in 1983. Walbridge received his master's degree in bilingual/cross-cultural education from California State University, San Bernadino, in 1993. He is also a senior trainer in California's Bilingual Teacher Training Program and a part-time instructor at Chapman University, specializing in bilingual and multicultural education.

Share Your Bright Ideas with Us!

We want to hear from you! Your valuable comments and suggestions will help us meet your current and future classroom needs.

Your name_____Date_____

School name_____Phone_____

School address_____

Grade level taught_____Subject area(s) taught_____Average class size_____

Where did you purchase this publication?_____

Was your salesperson knowledgeable about this product?   Yes_____   No_____

What monies were used to purchase this product?

___School supplemental budget   ___Federal/state funding   ___Personal

Please "grade" this Walch publication according to the following criteria:

Quality of service you received when purchasing ....A   B   C   D   F
Ease of use..A   B   C   D   F
Quality of content...A   B   C   D   F
Page layout ....A   B   C   D   F
Organization of material ....A   B   C   D   F
Suitability for grade level ....A   B   C   D   F
Instructional value...A   B   C   D   F

COMMENTS:_____

_____

What specific supplemental materials would help you meet your current—or future—instructional needs?

_____

Have you used other Walch publications? If so, which ones?_____

May we use your comments in upcoming communications?   ___Yes   ___No

Please **FAX** this completed form to **207-772-3105**, or mail it to:

Product Development, J.Weston Walch, Publisher, P.O. Box 658, Portland, ME 04104-0658

We will send you a **FREE GIFT** as our way of thanking you for your feedback.   **THANK YOU!**